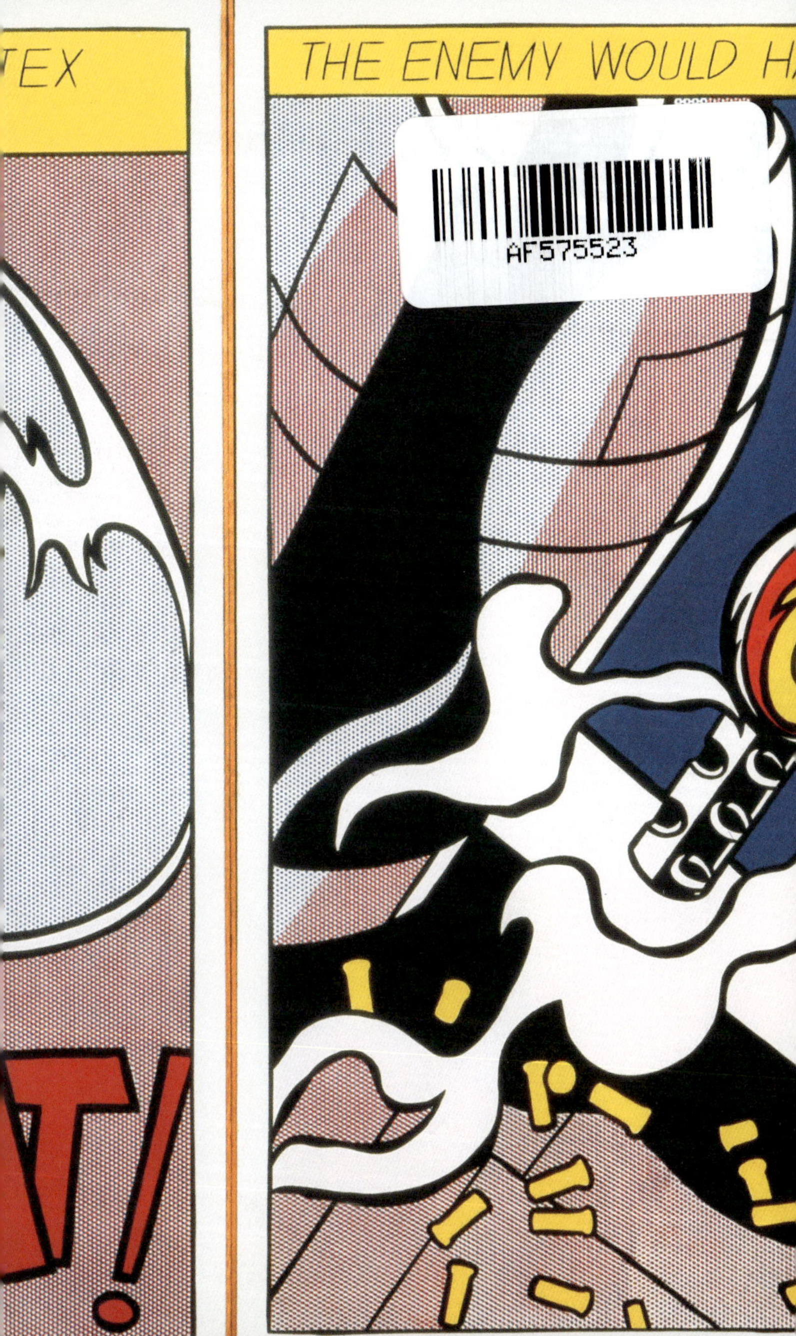
TEX
THE ENEMY WOULD
T!

Lucy R. Lippard is an internationally renowned activist, feminist, art critic and curator. She is known particularly for her work on contemporary art, including the seminal publication *Six Years: The Dematerialization of the Art Object* (1973), and more recently for her writing on environmental art. She was a founding member of the Art Workers Coalition, which campaigned for improved working conditions for artists, and of the feminist art collective and journal *Heresies*. She is also a co-founder of the New York artist publisher and art bookshop Printed Matter. Among many accolades, in 2015 she received the College Art Association's Distinguished Lifetime Achievement Award for Writing on Art.

POCKET PERSPECTIVES

Surprising, questioning, challenging, enriching: the Pocket Perspectives series presents timeless works by writers and thinkers who have shaped the conversation across the arts, visual culture and history. Celebrating the undiminished vitality of their ideas today, these covetable and collectable books embody the best of Thames & Hudson.

LUCY R. LIPPARD ON POP ART

With 34 illustrations

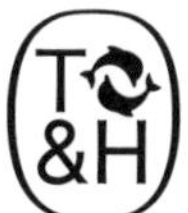

This book consists of extracts from *Pop Art* by Lucy R. Lippard, originally published in the World of Art series by Thames & Hudson in 1966.

Front cover and endpapers: Roy Lichtenstein, *As I Opened Fire...*, 1964. Acrylic, oil, graphite pencil on canvas, each panel 174 × 143.5 (68⅝ × 56½ in). Stedelijk Museum Amsterdam. Photo SuperStock/DeAgostini. © Estate of Roy Lichtenstein/DACS 2024

First published in the United Kingdom in 1966 under the title *Pop Art* by Thames & Hudson Ltd, London, 181A High Holborn, London WC1V 7QX

First published in the United States of America in 1966 under the title *Pop Art*, part of the Praeger World of Art series, published by Frederick A. Praeger, Inc., Publishers

This abridged edition published in the United Kingdom in 2024 by Thames & Hudson Ltd, London

This abridged edition published in the United States of America in 2024 by Thames & Hudson Inc., 500 Fifth Avenue, New York, New York 10110

British Library Cataloguing-in-Publication Data
A catalogue record for this book is available from the British Library

Library of Congress Control Number 2024934377

ISBN 978-0-500-02867-4

Printed in China by Shenzhen Reliance Printing Co. Ltd

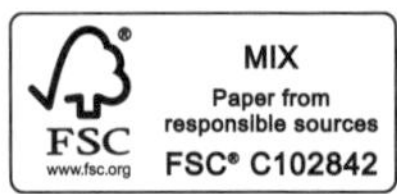

CONTENTS

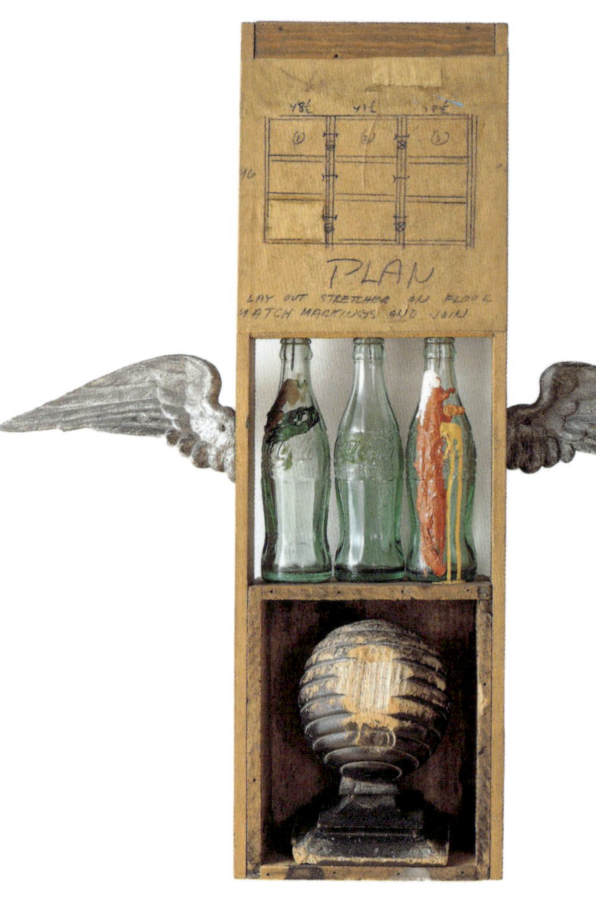

1. Robert Rauschenberg, *Coca-Cola Plan*, 1958.
Graphite on paper, oil on three Coca-Cola bottles, wood newel cap and cast metal wings on wood structure

PREFACE

Pop Art, my second book, was initiated in the early 1960s by The Art Digest Inc., who I think had in mind something very different. I was still in my twenties when it was published, and I'd been on the periphery of the so-called art world for a few years, although by that time I was more committed to so-called Minimalism and Conceptual Art and was falling for what I called Eccentric Abstraction, with its premonitions of feminist art. Pop was no longer new, but still popular. It is strange to find Pop Art – a celebration of consumerism and by proxy, capitalism – of interest almost sixty years later, in such very different times, confirming that what I recall as an exciting new experience is now art history.

Lucy R. Lippard

INTRODUCTION

POP ART is an American phenomenon that departs from the cliché of big, bold, raw America that became current when Abstract Expressionism triumphed internationally. It was born twice: first in England and then again, independently, in New York. At its second birth, Pop proved instantly appealing to young people the world over, who reacted enthusiastically to both the hot and the cool implications of such a direct idiom; it attracted a middle-aged generation that looked anxiously to youth for its excitement in the arts and entertainment, as well as those of all ages who recognized its formal validity. Pop Art itself was not a product of the discothèque era, but its reception was. More important, Pop is a hybrid, the product of two abstraction-dominated decades, and, as such, is the heir to an abstract rather than a figurative tradition. Pop Art has more in common with the American 'post-painterly abstraction' of Ellsworth Kelly or Kenneth Noland than with contemporary realism. When Pop first emerged in England, America, and Europe, raised eyebrows and indignation were accompanied by a profound disappointment on the part of many artists and critics. This unexpected outcome of a decade of Abstract Expressionism (or *Tachisme, art autre, l'art informel*) was hardly a welcome one, since it dashed hopes for the rise of a 'new humanism', known as the 'New Image of Man' in America and 'New Figuration' in Europe. Man might make an occasional appearance in Pop canvases, but only as a robot remotely controlled by the Consumers' Index, or as a sentimentalized parody of the ideal. For other observers, however, such a brash and uncritical reflection of our environment was a breath of fresh air.

Pop was not a grass-roots movement in any country, nor was it an international fusion of styles. Its standards were not determined by regionalism so much as by a widespread decision to approach the contemporary world with a positive rather than a negative attitude. Despite its carnival aspects, its orgiastic colour and giant scale, Pop Art's alternative to the emotional and technical impastoes of its immediate predecessor was clearly based on a tough, no-nonsense, no-preciosity, no-refinement standard appropriate to the 1960s. The choice of a 'teenage culture' as subject matter contains an element of hostility towards contemporary values rather than complacency; it marks a new detachment from the accepted channels of art. Yet Pop is nowhere a nihilist trend. In Europe the manifestations related to Pop tend to have sociological intentions frowned upon in America and England, but the underlying mood everywhere seems one of determined optimism – optimism against odds, an optimism not always recognizable to those viewers who do not share it. Andy Warhol was criticized in the early days of Pop because he said he wanted to be a machine. This was misunderstood by a society whose long-standing values are threatened by mechanization. Warhol's statement, like his art, is a challenge rather than a defeat, articulately accepted by G. R. Swenson, who wrote, 'Art criticism has generally refused to say that an object can be equated with a meaningful or aesthetic feeling, particularly if the object has a brand name. Yet, in a way, abstract art tries to be an object which we can equate with the private feelings of an artist. Andy Warhol presents objects we can equate with the public feelings of an artist. Many people are disturbed by...the trend towards de-personalization in the arts.... They fear the implications of a technological society.... A great deal that is good and valuable about our lives is that which is public and shared with the community. It is the most common clichés, the most common stock responses which we must deal with first if we are to come to some understanding of the new possibilities available to us in this brave and not altogether hopeless new world.'[1]

Yet for the individual artists, the Pop style was simply a way to embark upon a personal artistic expression that would owe little to prevailing modes. At first, largely unaware of their colleagues in the same city or in other countries, several isolated New York artists hit upon a common style by accident. It was in the air. Despite the eventual rapport between artists in Europe, America, and England, the mature Pop idiom is special to America – particularly New York and Los Angeles. Hard-core Pop Art is essentially a product of America's long-finned, big-breasted, one-born-every-minute society, its advantages of being more involved with the future than with the past. Iconographically, however, there were a great many precedents – European as well as American – for Pop subject matter. Some fifty years had passed since the seeds of Pop were sown by Cubist collage; in retrospect it is amazing that commercial subject matter had not been 'discovered' as the total basis for fine art long before this.

Folk artists of all nations have made use of commercial materials and emblems. In Europe, leading fine artists have included them since at least 1912. Nevertheless, Pop is not related to the extravagant 'modernism' of the Futurists, the sterile formalism of Purists Ozenfant and Le Corbusier, or the 'object portraits' of Picabia published in *291*, or Max Ernst's slightly altered pages from a wholesale hat catalogue. Among the American forebears, the flag gates, nineteenth-century trade signs, whimsies, and weather-vanes of folk art provide amusing counterparts to Pop Art but are unimportant as sources. Signs were used by the artists of the 1930s, both by painters and by photographers like Walker Evans and Rudolph Burckhardt, either as detail or documentation. The most direct parallel is Stuart Davis, whose *Lucky Strike* package of 1921 is the most widely mentioned prototype. It presents a single commercial image as its entire subject, but it is rearranged in a stylized Cubist framework. More to the point, and more direct, is his 1924 *Odol*, its labelled disinfectant bottle plainly visible and inscribed: 'It Purifies.' As Davis' art matured, he further abstracted the signs and lettering of an urban environment and put them to the service of a more forceful and generalized scheme. His abstract painting style, rather than his early work, may well have been a catalyst for the American Pop artists, along with the late cut-outs of Matisse, also shown in New York around 1960.

It is a mistake to attribute the emergence of Pop – in England and America at any rate – wholly to historical influences. The impetus is a contemporary one, as is the style. Nevertheless, in theory the ideas of two European masters are probably the most valid prototypes. If Fernand Léger and Marcel Duchamp did not directly influence the younger artists, they helped to mould the aesthetic situation in which Pop was possible. The inheritors of the Duchamp and Léger traditions diverged into two streams, which could be said to make up a superficial division of modern art, and it was the meeting of these two streams in New York in the late 1950s that decided the new trend. Léger, once a Purist, represents the 'clean', or neat, classical stream, while Duchamp's successors – the Dadaists, Surrealists, Assemblagists, and Nouveaux Réalistes – represent the 'dirty', or conglomerate, romantic stream. As intellectually impersonal as Léger was emotionally impersonal, from 1913 Duchamp showed his Olympian detachment by the selection of ready-made objects that were neither very attractive (at that time) nor very shocking (with the exception of R. Mutt's 1917 *Fountain* urinal and the mustached and goateed Mona Lisa entitled *L.H.O.O.Q.*). Many of his heirs went to extremes, but Duchamp has remained aloof. The ready-mades were given little formal attention at the time they were conceived; they were pawns in a cerebral exercise in which potential art status was conferred, or imposed, by Duchamp through sheer force of will. Time has since made the transformation that he refused to make, and objects originally intended in defiance of the prevailing domination of abstraction and formalism now seem as abstract as any contemporary work.

Léger, on the other hand, was nothing if not *engagé*, despite the Purist bias of his style. Viewing the machine as significant form – unlike the Futurists (and perhaps Duchamp too), for whom it was a love object – Léger expressed a great and modern interest in such things as superhighways, window display, advertising art, and that epitome of Americanism: Chicago. 'Every day modern industry creates objects which have an incontestable plastic value', he wrote, paralleling Duchamp's instinct for the ready-made. 'The spirit of these objects dominates the period.'[2] In another article he discussed 'the seductive shop windows where the isolated objects cause the prospective purchaser to halt: the new realism'. Noting that in the *bals musettes* in Paris one found airplane propellers hanging on the walls for decoration, he prophetically stated: 'It would require no great effort for the masses to be brought to feel and to understand the new realism, which has its origins in modern life itself, the continuing phenomena of life, under the influence of manufactured and geometrical objects, transposed to a realm where the imagination and the real meet and interlace.'[3]

In his film *Ballet mécanique* (1924), Léger even anticipated the technique of Pop Art: 'To isolate the object or the fragment of an object and to present it on the screen in close-ups of the largest possible scale.

Enormous enlargement of an object or fragment gives it a personality it never had before and in this way it can become a vehicle of entirely new lyric and plastic power.'[4] Still, the time was not yet ripe, and for all his intuitive understanding of urban art, and his own belief that he was the most 'American' of painters, Léger remained a Cubist, and French. While his robust forms, metallic surfaces, mechanical line, garish colour, and clear, schematic, often heavy-handed style are reflected in Pop Art – above all, in Lichtenstein's painting – conceptually they are miles apart. Despite his talk about depersonalization, Léger was a naïve idealist, even a social realist. Duchamp's irony and metaphysical cynicism hold much more attraction for the artists of the 1960s. Whatever Léger did he still considered himself an artist; Duchamp, for a time, was outside of art, closer to the 'real world' that the Pop artists extol.

Around 1958 the ideas of Duchamp and orthodox Surrealism as sifted through Abstract Expressionism began to merge. The initial result was the motley Assemblage trend in America, and Pierre Restany's *Nouveau Réalisme* and its offshoots in Europe. In New York, where Duchamp had been living off and on since 1914, Robert Rauschenberg and Jasper Johns had significant one-man shows at the Leo Castelli Gallery, providing the links, in that order, to Pop Art. Neither of these men is a Pop Artist in style or subject matter, though they have influenced and sympathized with Pop. Both of them were more or less affected by close association with the composer John Cage, who has been given credit (often exaggerated) for being the primary source of Pop Art. Rauschenberg had been at

Black Mountain College when Cage was there, and had participated in what is now called the 'first Happening'. Cage's ideas owe a good deal to Zen Buddhism and much less to Dada; his breakdown of distinctions between chosen and accidental sounds was undoubtedly the source of Rauschenberg's widely quoted remark that he wanted to work 'in the gap between life and art', as well as of his fondness for iconoclastic gestures. The most famous of these gestures were the duplication, to the last detail, of an 'Eisenhower combine'; the acquisition from de Kooning of a de Kooning drawing which was then erased, with some difficulty, and exhibited as 'Erased de Kooning by Robert Rauschenberg'; and the cabled reply to a request to make Iris Clert's portrait, which read: 'This is a portrait of Iris Clert if I say so.'

Rauschenberg's gestures span both Duchamp's exacting conceptualism, and statements of Cage's like: 'Ideas are one thing and what happens another.'[5] Later, when Warhol began to use commercial silkscreen techniques of reproducing photographs on canvas, Rauschenberg also employed them to replace his more awkward frottage transfer process. Yet his art has remained highly personal, rough, and abstract. Commercial images, photographs, and signs are not used specifically but are left in poetic suspension. Rauschenberg's importance to the further development of the art of common objects was his demonstration that the presence of blatantly descriptive images, intact, need not preclude an abstract solution.

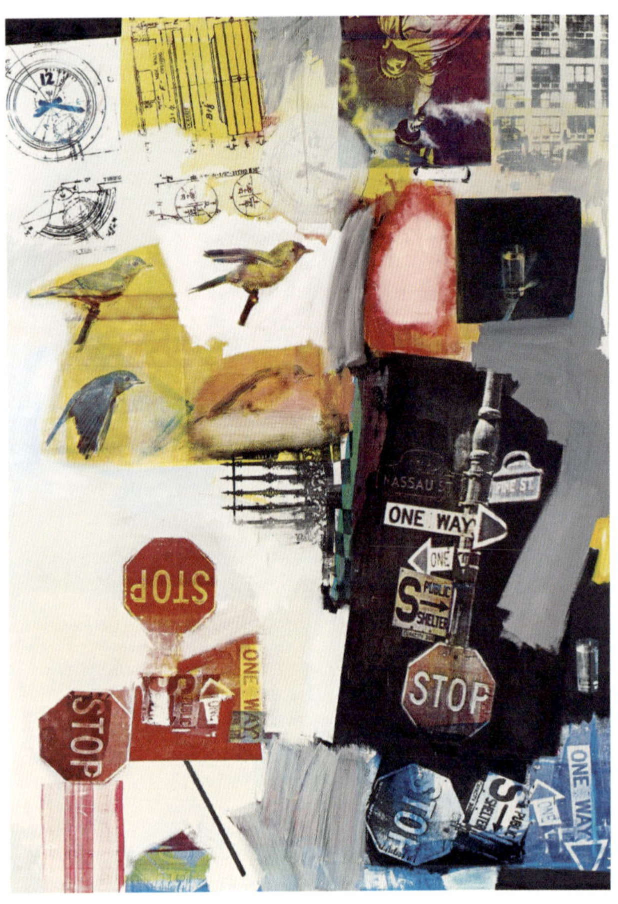

2. Robert Rauschenberg, *Overdrive*, 1963.
Oil and silkscreen ink on canvas

NEW YORK POP

THERE ARE SO MANY misconceptions about what is or is not Pop Art that for the purpose of the following discussion I should say that I admit to only five hard-core Pop artists in New York, and a few more on the West Coast and in England. They all employ more or less hard-edge, commercial techniques and colours to convey their unmistakably popular, representational images, but what they do stylistically with these characteristics is not necessarily similar. The New York five, in order of their commitment to these principles, are: Andy Warhol, Roy Lichtenstein, Tom Wesselmann, James Rosenquist, and Claes Oldenburg. If Pop Art is not a movement, with manifestoes and group demonstrations, it is at least a relatively cohesive tendency. The artists who originated the idiom are still the leading practitioners; the influence has spread, and Pop boasts not only a valid second wave, but also a generally imitative and incompetent third wave, not to mention the varied related European manifestations discussed later.

The real point of departure for Pop Art in New York was the work of Jasper Johns. His sense of pictorial irony is related to that of Duchamp, but like the majority of the best American painters, Johns is a painter first and an ideologist second. 'My idea has always been that in painting the way ideas are conveyed is through the way it looks and I see no way to avoid that, and I don't think Duchamp can either', he said in 1964.[6] Closely associated with Rauschenberg – who lived in the same building as he in the mid-1950s – Johns departed from his colleague's fusion of real, three-dimensional object and abstraction by depersonalizing his own action-painting techniques. A regular, almost patterned (though still delicate) brush-stroke was used to veil the single flag, target, or numbers depicted. Through the 'crisis of identity' raised by a two-dimensional painting portraying a two-dimensional object, Johns encompassed three major streams of abstract art: the Abstract Expressionist surface, the simplified composition of non-relational or emblematic art, and the post-Surrealist Assemblage. Duchamp had made the ready-made object into art; now Johns went further and made the object into a painting, challenging the mainline collage tradition in which the actual common object or picture was added to the surface, fragmented, disguised, or otherwise subjugated to a foreign aesthetic. He invaded the previously inviolate area of 'pure painting'. Whereas assemblages of all kinds, in their imperfect synthesis of motif and treatment, *had* acted 'in the gap' between life and art, Johns neutralized that gap. Once it was realized that the question 'Is it a flag or is it a painting?' had no answer – was not important – the way was wide open to Pop Art.

Between Johns' initial employment of single two-dimensional popular motifs and the emergence of hard-core Pop Art, came Assemblage. Still confused with Pop Art, Assemblage is a broad term for three-dimensional

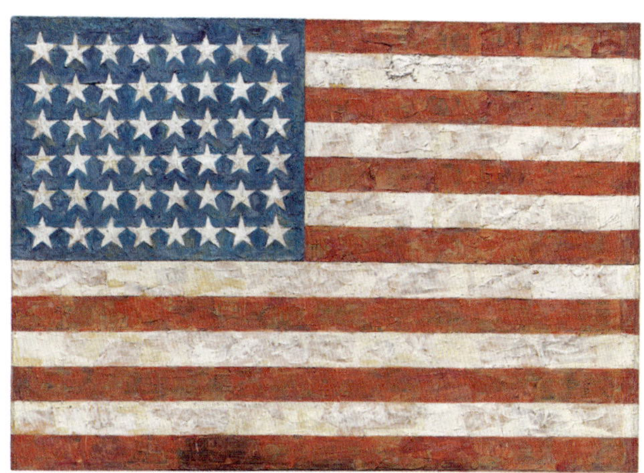

3. Jasper Johns, *Flag*, 1954–55. Encaustic, oil, and collage on fabric mounted on plywood, three panels collage or collage sculpture, using objects instead of pasted papers. It took its name and its cohesiveness from William C. Seitz's 'Art of Assemblage' exhibition at the Museum of Modern Art in the fall of 1961. A comprehensive and historical round-up of the many aspects of 'junk culture', the broad collage concept, and aspects of post-Abstract Expressionism, it was received as the beginning of a trend when in fact it was the end. By presenting an exhaustive survey of the additive tradition, the exhibition virtually killed Assemblage and prepared the way for a new art.

What Seitz called our 'collage environment' – dizzying signs, lights, advertisements, commercials, automobile graveyards, slum detritus, and 'new antiques' – had fascinated artists and poets since Apollinaire's day. It emerged as a major instead of a minor trend during the 1950s. In New York, Willem de Kooning superimposed a collage mouth from a magazine (the T-zone of a Camel cigarette ad) on one of his oil *Women* studies in 1950. In Chicago, H. C. Westermann was among the first to eschew nostalgia and make such popular objects look new; Oldenburg, who lived there at the time, has acknowledged the influence of Westermann's laminated wooden structures containing bottle tops and Times Square trivia, as well as of George Cohen's and June Leaf's interest in popular culture.[7] As far back as 1948, William Copley (CPLY) had painted flat American flags that filled the canvas. Since then he has made witty and erotic use of cartoon balloons and narrative techniques. In 1958 Johns had painted over the comic strip 'Alley Oop', and on the West Coast others were heading the same way.

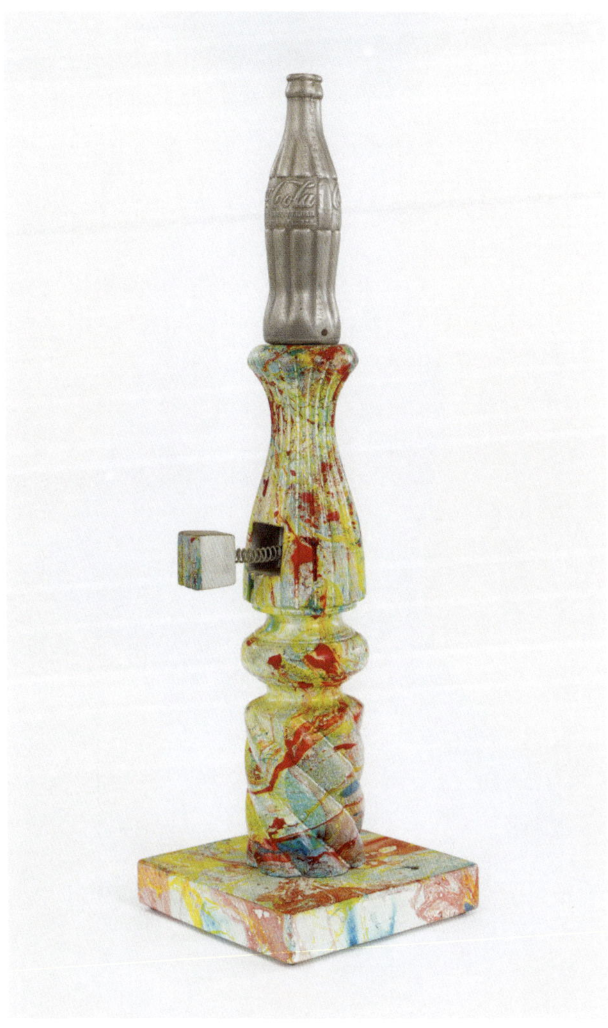

4. H.C. Westermann, *Pillar of Truth*, 1962. Red oak, pine, walnut, enamel, cast aluminium, metal spring

Integral to this increasing emphasis on the non-picturesque and non-associative aspects of commercial raw materials was a growing disdain for sentiment, and even for sensitivity, which, with anecdotalism, was a platform for the so-called humanist schools – from the social realism of the 1930s to the current Bacon-derived figuration. Jim Dine announced that he had stopped dealing with found objects because 'there was too much of other people's mystery in them'.[8] In part this attitude arose from the restlessness of a younger generation forced to follow in the giant footsteps of Pollock, Kline, and de Kooning. When Pop first arrived, it was pointed out that the reigning New York School had also felt strongly about Pop subject matter. Elaine de Kooning said of Kline in 1962: 'The American style as he saw it – with a fan's zest and expertise – had an element of the comic; the big brash breezy gesture that, carried to its extreme, becomes a not-unconscious parody of itself, as in the design of a Cadillac or the cut of a zootsuit...the forceful sentimentality of Tin Pan Alley songs.'[9]

Pop was indeed a fulfilment of such attitudes, couched in the unexpected vocabulary of a new generation. After the first burst of anti-Abstract Expressionist diatribes early in 1962 (often exaggerated or oversimplified statements put into the Pop artists' mouths by earnest critics), it became evident that this withdrawal from the principles of Abstract Expressionism was largely based on admiration and respect for that movement: it had been done too well to continue. None the less, abstraction was the mode of the times and it was up to the artists to discover new angles from which to approach it. While the older painters were generally repelled by the rise of Pop, the 'cool' strain of Abstract Expressionism – Rothko, Still, and especially Barnett Newman – had become the main force in the new abstraction; aspects of this style seemed equally applicable to the depiction of anonymous objects with no history and no evocative impedimenta.

Included in the 'Assemblage' exhibition were Lucas Samaras and George Brecht from the downtown Reuben Gallery, which also represented Oldenburg, Red Grooms, Jim Dine, Rosalyn Drexler, and Robert Whitman. The cradle of Pop and *avant-garde* art on the Lower East Side, the Reuben specialized in an impermanent, perishable gutter art that went beyond Surrealism in its involvement with urban industrial subject matter for its own sake. Some of the first Happenings (environmental syntheses of theatre and the visual arts) were performed there, and the group was closely associated with the prolific father of that medium – Allan Kaprow – and with other artists then teaching at Rutgers University: Watts, Segal, and Lichtenstein. Many of them had been active in the 1952–59 Hansa co-operative gallery which, through Richard Bellamy's later Green Gallery, also had ties to Pop Art's origins. The Reuben inherited much of its ambiance, as well as its members, from the Hansa, and its artists formed the heart of two uptown exhibitions held at the Martha Jackson Gallery: 'New Forms, New Media' (1960) and 'Environments, Situations, Spaces' (1961). Lichtenstein has said that he was more influenced by Kaprow and this trend than by Johns and Rauschenberg.[10]

In 1959, Oldenburg's *The Street*, together with Dine's *The House* – both environments – were presented at the Judson Gallery, another early headquarters. In the spring of 1961, Robert Indiana, Stephen Durkee, and Richard Smith held an obscure exhibition of 'premiums' at the Studio for Dance. It was reviewed only by G.R. Swenson, who noted that they 'took the world too seriously not to be amused by it'.[11] Included were Indiana's wooden constructions from raw beams with stencilled letters and 'American' insignia, inspired by a circular stencil found in his former sail loft on Coenties Slip. Durkee, whose connection with Pop was tenuous and brief, employed some commercial motifs, including a hand painted by a professional sign painter – an act of disavowal also made by Duchamp in his famous *Tu m'* of 1918. Smith, an Englishman living in New York, worked in a fundamentally abstract style based on enlarged images of objects – a watch or a cigarette packet. His work owed its glamorous colour and shimmering surface to chic photographic magazine advertising, its scale and approach to Newman and Rothko.[12] While these three artists were ultimately non-objective painters, they were among the strongest exponents of the pre-Pop message. Others using popular objects in their work at that time were George Brecht, who filled his boxes and medicine chests with plastic toys and miscellany, and Ray Johnson, who sends and receives his collage materials through the mail, thereby using the US postal service as his medium for communicating a conglomeration of ideas – some of them related to Pop. Dan Flavin mounted crushed tin cans on painterly grounds;

Yayoi Kusama anticipated Warhol's repeated rows of soup cans, money, green stamps, and photographs with her own repeated rows of mailing stickers used non-objectively; Robert Watts and Robert Morris employed objects in a complex, conceptual manner more closely related to Duchamp. By 1959 Andy Warhol was concentrating on single comic-book characters in a drippy New York School technique, Lichtenstein was working from animated cartoon strips, Rosenquist had made his single transitional painting between a greyed Abstract Expressionist mode and the billboard style, Oldenburg had made the phallic *Ray Guns* commemorating his Ray Gun ('sounds like New York backwards') Manufacturing Company, and Wesselmann, who had shared a show at Judson with Dine in 1958, was making his 'portrait collages'.

With these and other events in the air, by the time of the 'Assemblage' exhibition the perceptive observer began to notice a gradual shift from the rusty, peeling, aged, and mellowed surface to a cleaner cut, simpler, more blaring, ordered, and 'cool' expression within the Assemblage trend. It also appeared in non-objective art with exhibitions of Ellsworth Kelly, Frank Stella, and Kenneth Noland, among others. In 1958–59 Jasper Johns had made a flashlight, light bulb, 'teeth' brush, and mouthed spectacles of sculpmetal; and flags, a light bulb, and painted Savarin can with brushes in it of bronze; in 1960 he made two hand-painted bronze Ballantine ale cans, in reply to de Kooning's crack that Leo Castelli could sell anything – even two beer cans. By 1961 these cans looked like the harbingers of a full-fledged trend.

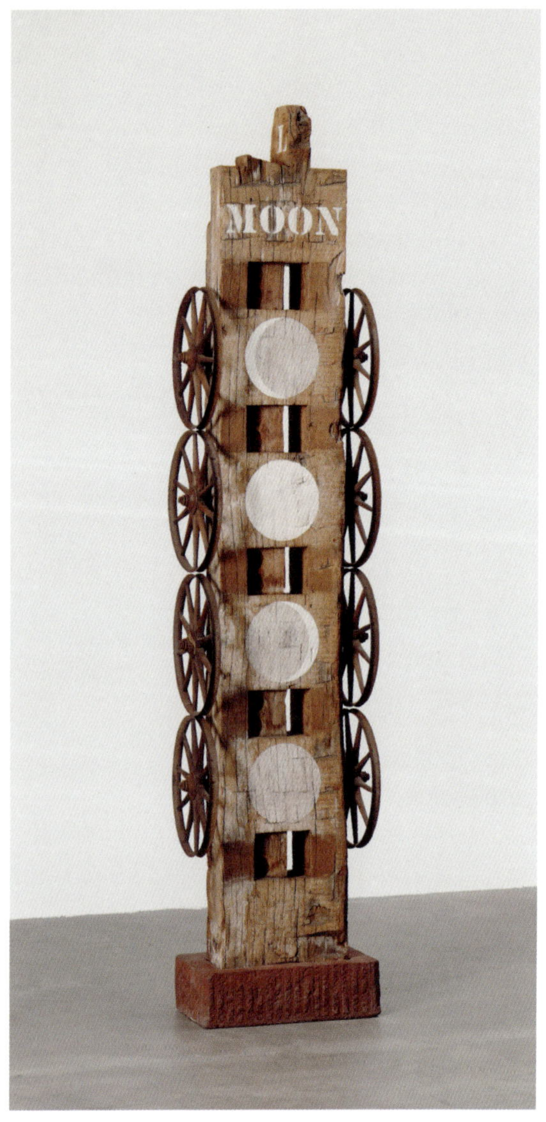
MOON

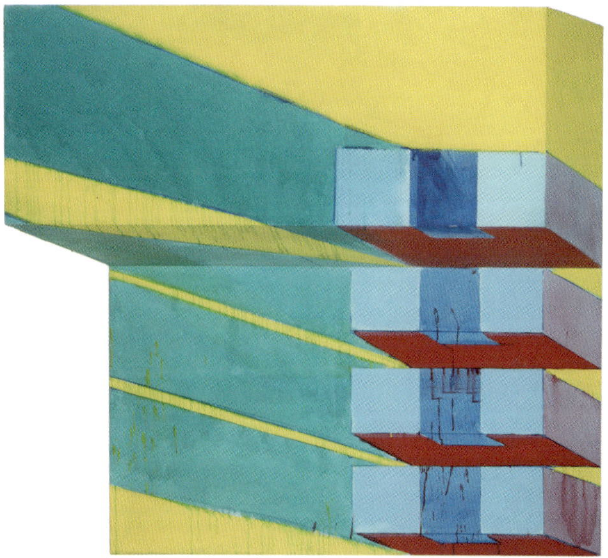

Opposite 5. Robert Indiana, *Moon*, 1960. Acrylic gesso on wood beam with wood-and-iron wheels and concrete

6. Richard Smith, *Quartet*, 1964. Oil on canvas

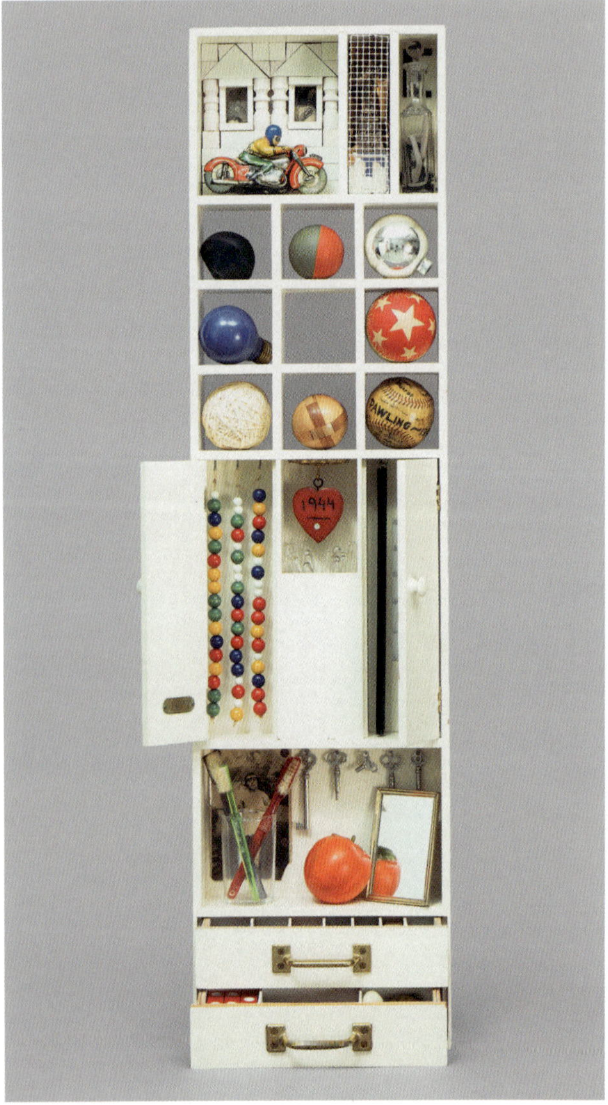
1944

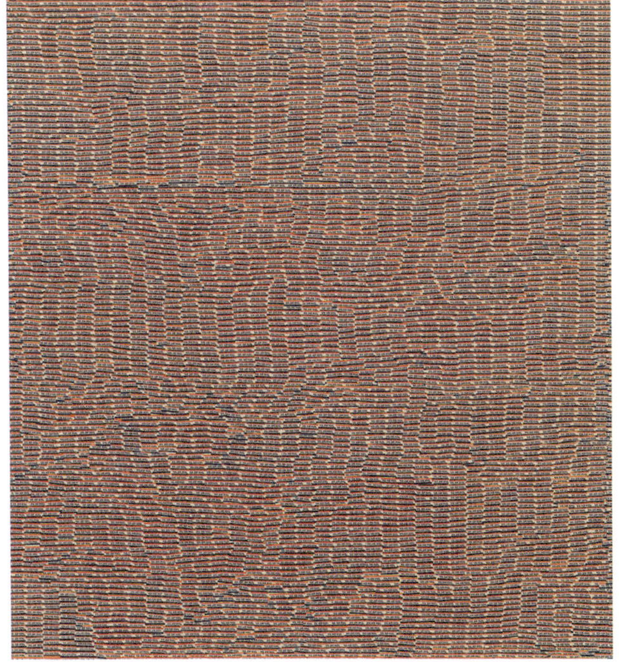

Opposite 7. George Brecht, *Repository*, 1961. Wall cabinet containing pocket watch, thermometer, plastic and rubber balls, baseball, plastic persimmon, 'Liberty' statuette, wood puzzle, toothbrushes, bottlecaps, house number, plastic worm, pocket mirror, light bulbs, keys, hardware and photographs

8. Yayoi Kusama, *Air Mail Stickers*, 1962. Collaged paper on canvas

But by the beginning of 1962, they looked like antiques in comparison with the newly emerged Pop Art. For the ale cans were clearly hand-painted, and in no way did they attempt to reproduce exactly the commercial labels, or even the exact size and shape of the actual cans; still more significant, they were on a bronze base – set apart as art. The ale cans share the technical ambiguity of Johns' early flags – the conflict of quasi-expressionist technique and commercial motif.

The next step was to bring these cans or similar objects still closer to reality by further eradicating the 'artistic' remnants. Johns himself did not go this far. One of the many reasons Johns is not and never was a Pop artist is that his subjects are not brand new. Their painterly surface rids them of the newly minted mass-produced aura typical of Pop. The patina of Johns' objects is neither sentimental nor picturesquely evocative, like that of some arsenic-and-old-lace Assemblagists, but it does connote use. Use in turn connotes the past, and the past, even the immediate past, evokes memories. Pop objects determinedly forgo the uniqueness acquired by time. They are not yet worn or left over. Every Campbell's soup can looks like every other Campbell's soup can since it has had no time to acquire character; every TV commercial on one channel at a given moment is the same, whether it is seen in Saugatuck or in Sioux City. The broad and instant appeal of Pop Art in America may indeed have been because the exposure to popular images is an experience shared by all Americans – young and old, urban and rural, from all backgrounds and all regions. The man in the White House is a Pop Art

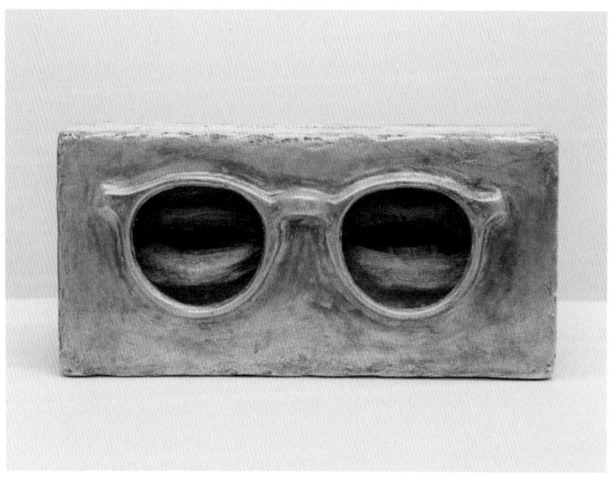

9. Jasper Johns, *The Critic Sees*, 1961.
Sculpmetal on plaster with glass

President – big, sentimental, plainspoken, and tough; 'See America First' is one of his dicta. For the sophisticated, even the new has a nostalgic attraction, recalling those palmy days when bicycles, baseball games, drive-ins, hot dogs, ice-cream sodas, and comics were the low-brow facts of life, uncomplicated by intellectual responsibility.

The works of Oldenburg, Wesselmann, Indiana, Smith, and Dine had been shown often, and group exhibitions had yielded glimpses of others moving in a similar direction. Around the spring of 1961, Richard Bellamy of the Green Gallery, and Ivan Karp and Leo Castelli of the Castelli Gallery (which already represented Rauschenberg and Johns) saw the works of Rosenquist, Lichtenstein, and Warhol, and, recognizing their importance, they also understood that these artists provided the missing link between Assemblage and hard-edge abstraction, and had independently arrived at something new. As well acquainted as anyone with what was going on in studios and galleries in New York, Bellamy, Karp, and Castelli were able to tie in their discoveries with other isolated instances. Robert Scull bought a Rosenquist and became the first collector to concentrate on Pop Art; he was soon followed by the Burton Tremaines, Philip Johnson, Harry Abrams, and others. By the beginning of 1962, Lichtenstein, Dine, and Rosenquist had had one-man shows, and the new art was in the open. It was called Neo-Dada, Commonism, OK Art, Common Image Art, Pop Culture, and various other labels – few complimentary. Finally the British term – Pop Art – triumphed, although it had been coined by Lawrence Alloway with reference to the sources of Pop Art (the comics, billboards, cowboy movies, etc.) rather than to their fine-art progeny.

It is rare that collectors and general public, *Life* and the *Ladies Home Journal* accept a new art before many critics and museums. Pop Art has given rise to a cult of liking that obscures the contribution it has made. Because it is easy to look at and often amusing, recognizable and therefore relaxing, Pop has been enjoyed and applauded on an extremely superficial level. This does not do justice to the five major artists discussed here, who are constantly reminding the public that they are not just Pop artists, but artists. 'Some of the worst things about Pop Art have come from its admirers', Tom Wesselmann complained in 1963. 'They begin to sound like some nostalgia cult – they really worship Marilyn Monroe or Coca-Cola. The importance people attach to things an artíst uses is irrelevant.... I use a billboard picture because it is a real, special representation of something, not because it is from a billboard. Advertising images excite me mainly because of what I can make from them.' And James Rosenquist has insisted that for him 'the subject matter isn't popular images, it isn't that at all'.[13]

Pop chose to depict everything previously considered unworthy of notice, let alone of art: every level of advertising, magazine and newspaper illustration, Times Square jokes, tasteless bric-à-brac and gaudy furnishings, ordinary clothes and foods, film stars, pin-ups, cartoons. Nothing was sacred, and the cheaper and more despicable the better. Nor were the time-honoured methods of creating art respected. Lichtenstein and Warhol did not even 'invent' their images, and it was generally agreed that they did nothing about them once they had selected them. The former used a projector to enlarge his sources, filled in the Ben Day dots with a screen, and had his baked-enamel paintings produced in multiple editions. Warhol hand-painted his 'products' at first but then began to silkscreen them by commercial techniques, hiring others to duplicate and even to execute his work; it too has appeared in editions. Wesselmann has a carpenter to complete his constructions, and Coosje van Bruggen, Oldenburg's wife, still does all the sewing, though now she has helpers. Rosenquist's industrial painting techniques, unpleasantly soft surfaces, and sweet white-based colours further enraged the *cognoscenti*. He was known as 'the billboard painter', and at first it was inferred (by *Time*) that he was not an artist at all, but an outdoor advertiser who had fallen on to a good thing. Roy Lichtenstein was called the 'comic-strip man' and *Life* billed him as 'the worst artist in the US'. Andy Warhol was 'the Campbell's soup guy' and titillated the experts by nonchalantly signing ordinary soup cans and selling them as souvenirs.

This was all a bitter pink pill for many people to swallow. They assumed that the intention in subjecting the viewer to such indignities could only be satirical. What else could it be? Surely there was no other reason to paint such vulgar images, from which all sensitive souls recoiled in horror. Critics and curators who endorsed Pop Art as an aggressively optimistic and original style were accused of jumping on the commercial bandwagon and trying to make their suspect allegiance respectable.

There is still a great hue and cry about the public being 'put on' by a diabolic artist-dealer-critic-collector cartel. At the same time, critics with reservations about the Pop contribution were accused by its protagonists of being reactionaries. Observers mistook the hard-sell techniques of the paintings' prototypes as representative of the artists' goals, and Pop was a sitting duck for much philistine and some genuinely witty adverse comment.

In the course of 1962, New York Pop really arrived. By autumn, Wesselmann, Oldenburg, Segal, Marisol and Warhol had had uptown exhibitions. Max Kozloff's mordant commentary on 'the new vulgarians' appeared in *Art International* in February; G. R. Swenson, one of Pop's earliest enthusiasts, wrote the first sympathetic article on 'the new sign painters', published in *Art News* in September. *Time, Newsweek*, and *Life* covered the new scandal in the spring of 1962 and have continued to give it space ever since. In the autumn, Pop was consecrated as fashionable by the Sidney Janis Gallery's 'New Realists' exhibition, an uneven, international conglomeration to which critical response was far from mild, and journalistic response delirious. Here the hard-core American Pop artists stood out from the Neo-Surrealist Europeans (from whom the exhibition title was borrowed), and it became clear that anything innovatory was provided by American – specifically New York – artists, with the British close behind. The 'Neo-Dada' label was applicable to much in this show but it was unfortunately imposed on Pop Art as well, since the assumption was that Pop's goal was satire.

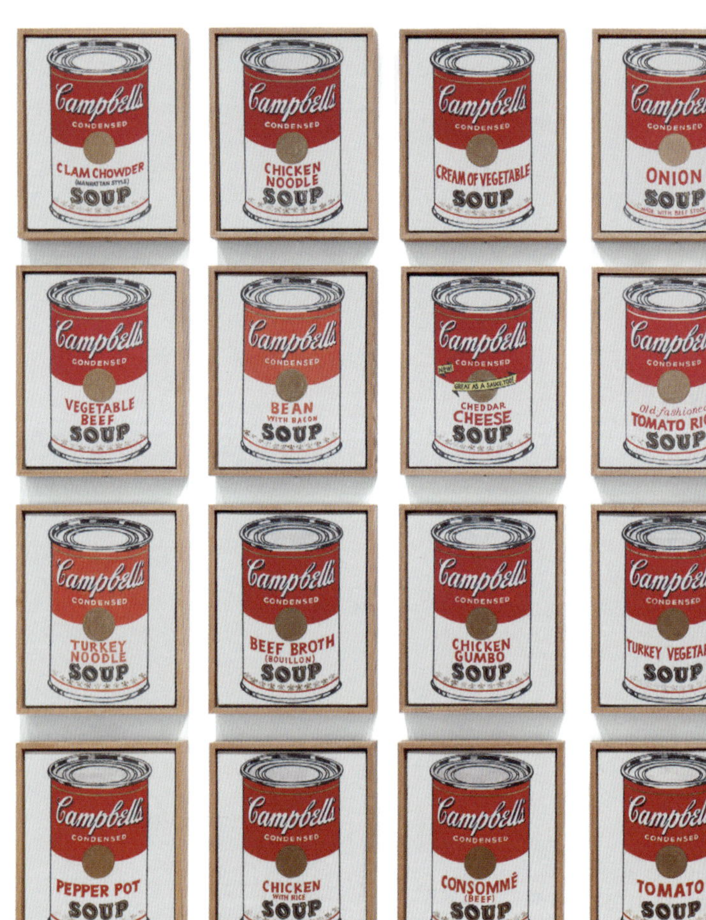

10. Andy Warhol, *Campbell's Soup Cans*, 1962.
Acrylic with metallic enamel paint on canvas, 32 panels

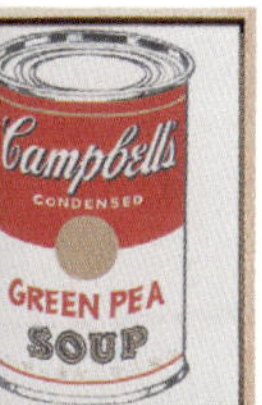
Campbell's
CONDENSED
GREEN PEA
SOUP

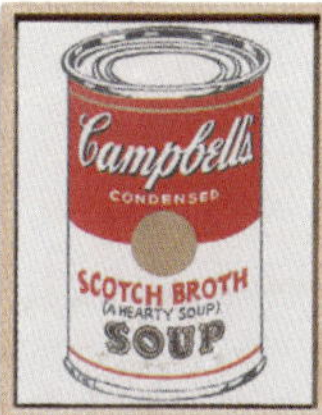
Campbell's
CONDENSED
SCOTCH BROTH
(A HEARTY SOUP)
SOUP

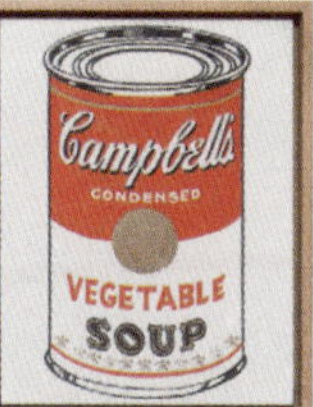
Campbell's
CONDENSED
VEGETABLE
SOUP

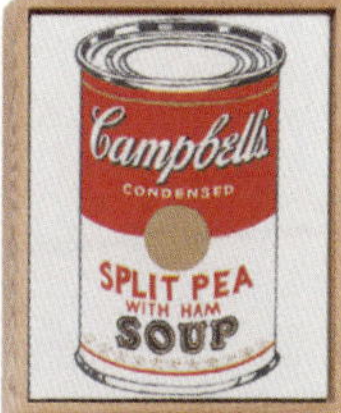
Campbell's
CONDENSED
SPLIT PEA
WITH HAM
SOUP

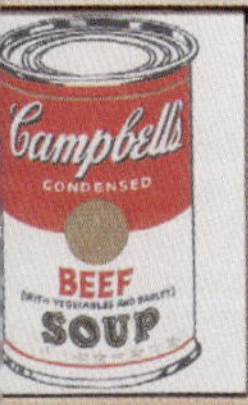
Campbell's
CONDENSED
BEEF
SOUP

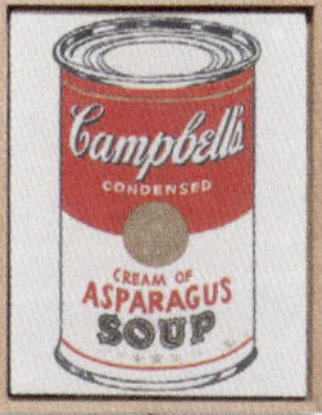
Campbell's
CONDENSED
CREAM OF
ASPARAGUS
SOUP

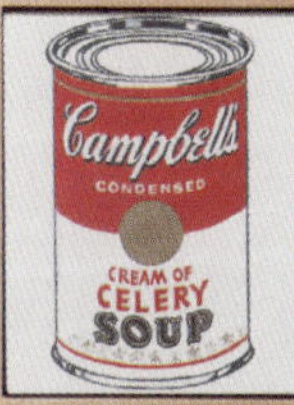
Campbell's
CONDENSED
CREAM OF
CELERY
SOUP

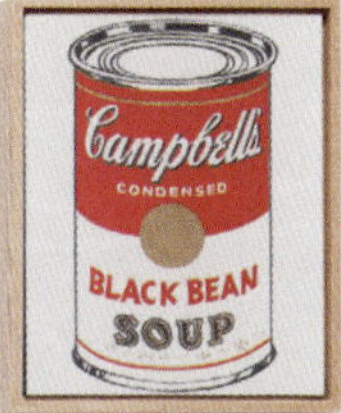
Campbell's
CONDENSED
BLACK BEAN
SOUP

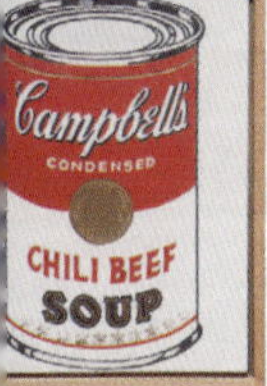
Campbell's
CONDENSED
CHILI BEEF
SOUP

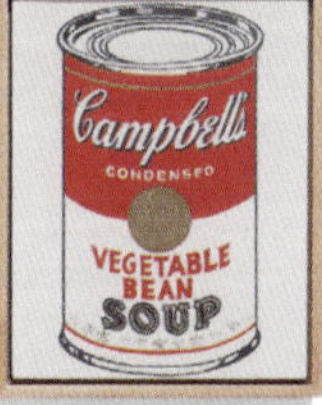
Campbell's
CONDENSED
VEGETABLE
BEAN
SOUP

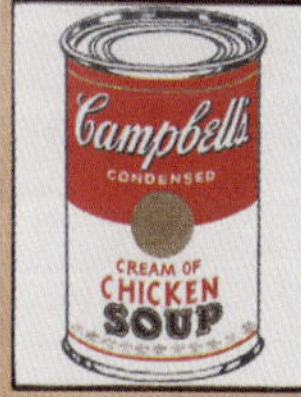
Campbell's
CONDENSED
CREAM OF
CHICKEN
SOUP

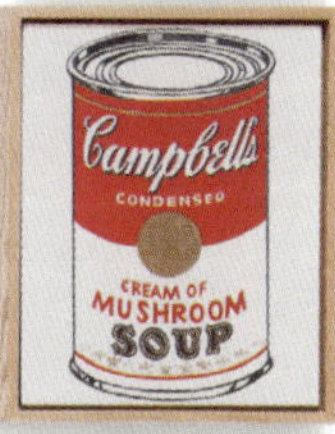
Campbell's
CONDENSED
CREAM OF
MUSHROOM
SOUP

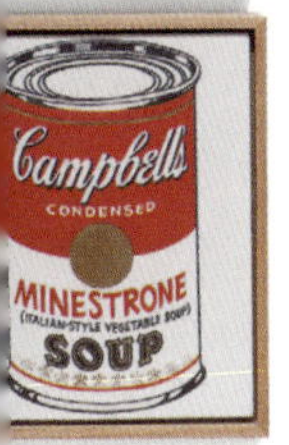
Campbell's
CONDENSED
MINESTRONE
SOUP

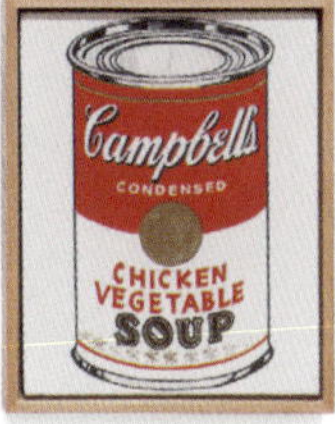
Campbell's
CONDENSED
CHICKEN
VEGETABLE
SOUP

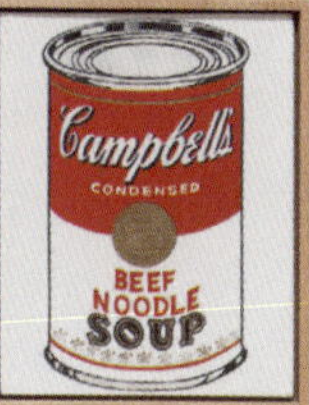
Campbell's
CONDENSED
BEEF
NOODLE
SOUP

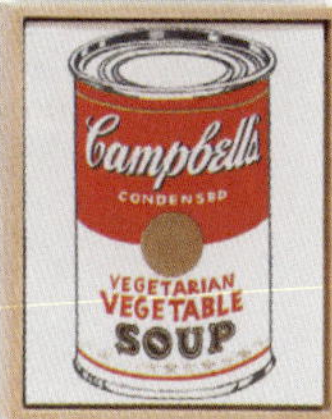
Campbell's
CONDENSED
VEGETARIAN
VEGETABLE
SOUP

It is still not widely understood that what seems to be satire and is often dismissed as complacent acceptance is in fact a new way of dealing with life and art. From the nineteenth-century realists to the Ash Can School, humble subjects were depicted; their humbleness was means to an anecdotal end. For each of the individual Pop artists the goal is different, yet for all of them it is divorced from story-telling or social comment. Some seek a high level of fantasy, some abstraction, some a strictly conceptual triumph. 'For me,' says Oldenburg, 'I have a very high idea of art. I'm still a romantic about that, but this process of humbling it is just to test it, to reduce everything to the same level and *then* see what you get.' These artists do not see themselves as destroyers of Art, but as the donors of a much-needed transfusion to counteract the effects of a rarified Abstract Expressionist atmosphere. 'Art since Cézanne has become extremely romantic and unrealistic, feeding on art; it is utopian,' said Lichtenstein. 'It has had less and less to do with the world; it looks inward.... Outside is the world. Pop Art looks out into the world; it appears to accept its environment, which is not good or bad, but different, another state of mind.' Indiana says of his *EAT* signs: 'The word "eat" is reassuring, it means not only food, but life. When a mother feeds her children, the process makes her indulgent, a giver of life, of love, of kindness.'[14] Thus despite the toughness of their approach, several of these artists consent to the metaphor that lurks behind even the most unyielding motifs. In a symposium at the Museum of Modern Art in 1962, Dore Ashton accused the Pop artists of banishing metaphor, but replied to her own complaint by adding that 'not an overcoat, not a Coca-Cola bottle, can resist the onslaught of the imagination. Metaphor is as natural to the imagination as saliva to the tongue'.[15]

Far from constituting laziness on the part of the artist who chooses such new-born objects to depict, an insistent emphasis on a single object, the present alone, takes both discipline and ingenuity. It is not easy to adhere to a stringent reduction of means without falling back into conventional beauties and emotions. As Roy Lichtenstein has said of his shift from animated cartoons to comic books 'with a more serious content, such as *Armed Forces at War* and *Teen Romance*, it was very difficult not to show everything I knew about a whole tradition. It was difficult not to be seduced by nuances of "good painting" '. To the charge of impersonalism levelled pejoratively at Pop Art, he replied: 'We think of the last generation as trying to reach their own subconscious while supposedly Pop artists are trying to get outside of the work. I want my work to look programmed or impersonal but I don't believe I'm being impersonal while I do it. Cézanne talked about losing himself. We tend to confuse the style of the finished work with the methods in which it was done. Every artist has disciplines of impersonality to enable him to become an artist in the first place.' Claes Oldenburg added that 'making impersonality the style characterizes Pop Art in a pure sense'.

The New York Pop artists are often asked whether or not they *like* their subjects. This, as Dorothy Seckler has noted, is as irrelevant as asking whether Cézanne liked apples, Géricault corpses, or Picasso guitars. Warhol alone benignly accepts everything; he has said that 'Pop Art is liking things'. Parody in Pop Art largely seems to depend upon the viewer's response, and is seldom the artist's intention; or if the satirical humour is intentional, it may be secondary to the point of the painting. If the viewer dislikes the subject matter, he will be repelled initially no matter how the artist has depicted it. The artist can only isolate the subject, present it in a hitherto unforeseen way so that the viewer has a chance to 'see it through new eyes' – a principle to which the Surrealists adhered by means of juxtaposition rather than pure isolation. Many of the Pop artists are excited about the jazzy, blaring, glaring, hectically 'fun' urban environment, about Times Square, Fourteenth Street, Coney Island, and cowboy movies. Enjoyment, however, does not mean wholesale endorsement any more than indifference means wholesale condemnation. I suspect that, like Lichtenstein, most of us like aspects of his subject matter. 'In parody,' he says, 'the implication is the perverse, and I feel that in my own work I don't mean it to be that. Because I don't dislike the work that I'm parodying… . The things that I have apparently parodied I actually admire.'

Nevertheless, the Pop artists do not naïvely idealize their subjects. They know what they are handling since they all have backgrounds in commercial art. Warhol was a successful fashion illustrator of shoes; Rosenquist learned billboard painting as a trade; Lichtenstein worked in design and display; Oldenburg in magazine illustration and design; and Wesselmann studied to be a cartoonist.

Yet all of them were artists first and foremost, devoting their energies to serious painting. They are aware of the continuing ambiguous relationship between commercial and fine art, and that there are still areas they have not touched in their work. They have all steered away from the slick advertisement that imitates the modern fine arts. The comics used by Lichtenstein are not up-to-date, as cartoonists have noted,[16] and are closer to the comics of the 1950s than to the less brash recent variety. Warhol does not utilize the tasteful advertisements of the sort that he himself once produced. The Brillo box, for instance, was designed by an Abstract Expressionist artist – James Harvey – but its effective design is directed at saleability rather than attractiveness. Wesselmann, like Warhol, is particularly fond of Del Monte labels because of their strong, simple, and slightly old-fashioned emblems. The 'clever' ads like Levy's Bread, the pretty ones like Modess, the chic ones like Smirnoff and Volkswagen, and the elegant ones from *Vogue* or *Harper's Bazaar* have not been used, because they have been created by men who can claim to be artists in their own right – Avedon, Stern, or Hiro. Such 'beautiful' and witty ads are usually based on exactly what Pop Art is getting away from: expert art-school design, striking but tasteful colour, asymmetrical composition, and Bauhaus to Abstract Expressionist iconography. It should be noted, incidentally, that some 'modern' advertisers are now returning to the stronger, old versions because of Pop.

Unlike Chardin, Courbet, and other realists who have been mentioned as prototypes, the Pop artists do not

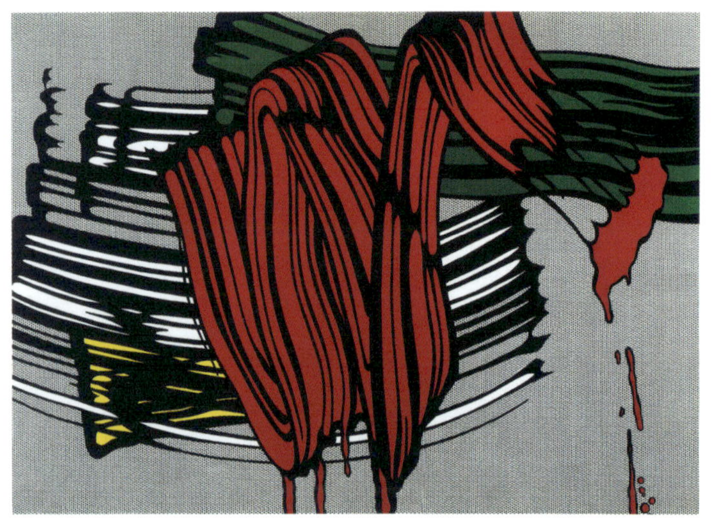

11. Roy Lichtenstein, *Big Painting No. 6*, 1965.
Acrylic and oil on canvas

simply portray common objects or take stylistic leads from folk cultures, but operate at one remove from actuality. Life as represented in the comic strips or advertisements bears little resemblance to real life. Already separated from life by the cellophane barrier of commercialism, Pop Art can function with detachment and still retain a hold on the emotional or sensorial reactions of the viewer. As Lichtenstein has said, 'the closer my work is to the original, the more threatening and critical the content'.[17] At the same time, it is the narrow distance between the 'original' and the Lichtenstein that provokes the tension and the great drama of his best work. For some reason, the problem of 'transformation' has been raised more often in regard to Lichtenstein than to Warhol, perhaps because Warhol's work is so ultimate in its rejection of involvement that it must be accepted as a *fait accompli*, while Lichtenstein's is still 'art' and therefore all the more irritating. Derived from small images in the first place – comic strips and the badly drawn, low-brow advertising images – Lichtenstein's work suffers even more than that of the other artists in reproduction, not because scale is the only change he has made from the original, but because the abstract use of space and colour as well as the immediate effect are drastically diminished and often totally invisible in reduced black-and-white illustrations. People have found his work especially odious in reproduction who might have had a far more favourable reaction to the painting itself. But Lichtenstein's is also a difficult art in that his humour and use of the found image is unexpectedly subtle for its obstreperous vehicle:

at times it is 'in' humour – based on references to friends or to other paintings. Examples are his four identical portraits of a grinning man, each of which bears a different title: *Portrait of Ivan Karp, Portrait of Allan Kaprow*, etc.; or the 1965 *Big Painting*, with the gestural swathes rendered in commercial harshness as a parody of action painting. And there are the notorious Lichtensteins in which impassive translations are made of well-known modern masterpieces – Cézanne's *Man With Folded Arms*, Picasso's *Woman With Flowered Hat*, a non-objective Mondrian. Even more extreme, and typically Pop, was a twice-removed painting – *after* a published diagram *after* a Cézanne canvas, whereby Lichtenstein went further than Duchamp had in 'decorating' the *Mona Lisa* (and provoked two irate articles by the author of the diagram – Erle Loran).[18] In a 1961 comic painting, a uniformed officer 'thinks': 'I am supposed to report to a Mr Bellamy. I wonder what he's like'; a sinister helmeted face glares out from another canvas, saying: 'What? Why did you ask that? What do you know about my image duplicator?'; in another, a limpid blonde gushes to her painter boyfriend: 'Why Brad, darling, this painting is a masterpiece! My, soon you'll have all of New York clamouring for your work!' Most of the Pop artists have injected similar sight gags or amusing verbal comment at one time or another, but humour is never paramount in their work, as it is not in Lichtenstein's. It is only to be hoped that the majority of their public is able to enjoy these moments without being too weighed down by the terrible possibility that it may not be Art if it's funny.

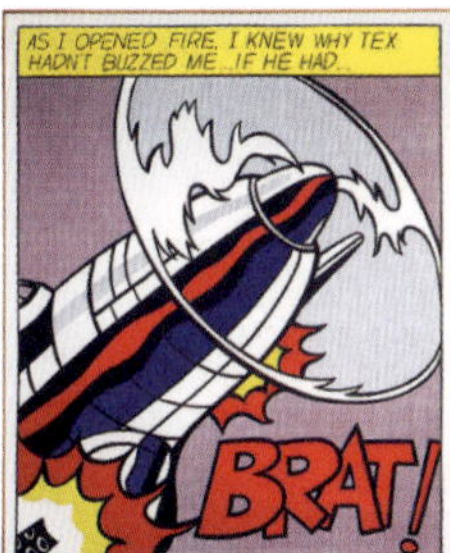

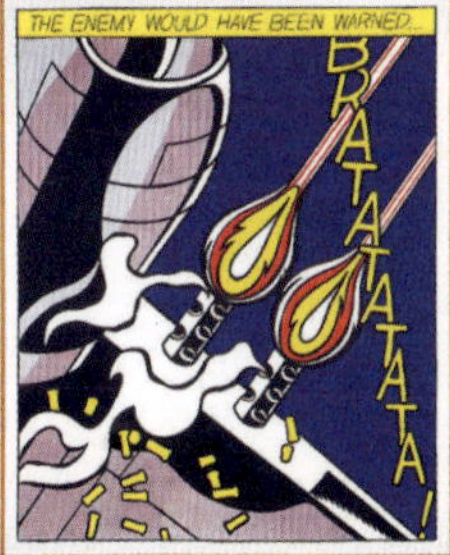

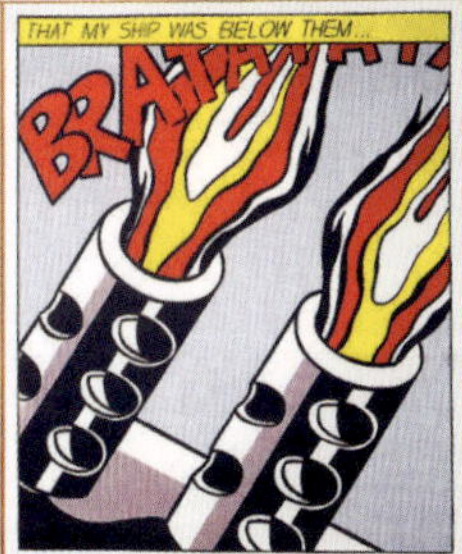

12. Roy Lichtenstein, *As I Opened Fire...*, 1964.
Acrylic, oil, graphite pencil on canvas

Many people have no doubt shared Leo Steinberg's experience when he was first confronted with the comic book paintings in January of 1962. 'In Lichtenstein's work', said Steinberg, 'the subject matter exists for me so intensely that I have been unable to get through to whatever painterly qualities there may be.'[19] Lichtenstein is excited by the 'highly emotional content, yet detached impersonal handling', of love, hate, or war in these cartoon images, but he finds their pictorial structures outweigh emotive considerations. To those who complain about lack of 'transformation', Lichtenstein has replied that art does not transform, 'it just plain forms. Artists have never worked with the model, just with the painting'. In a published comic-strip or book, the images have 'shapes but there has been no effort to make them intensely unified. The purpose is different; one intends to depict and I intend to unify'. Unification is in fact the key to his work. He omits distracting details, lines, figures, or words that destroy form in his sources, and presents that form, rearranged, in its ultimate clarity. He makes of a confusing narrative sequence a clear-cut well-knit design in which the 'story' is so blatant that it can be instantly appreciated for its humour, or horror, and as instantly dismissed. For the professional comic artists, stylization is a short-cut, not an abstracting device; where they interpret naturalism by shorthand only to make that naturalism more rapidly legible, Lichtenstein generalizes, reduces, and simplifies. It is not necessary to compare canvas and source to enjoy the painting, but when one does, the differences are explicit and enlightening.

Perhaps the closer the Pop artist is to real life (as opposed to the artificial life of the mass media), the more he verges on satire and humanism. Lichtenstein and Warhol keep their distance. But Oldenburg, who is 'for an art that takes its form from the lines of life, that twists and extends impossibly and accumulates and spits and drips and is sweet and stupid as life itself',[20] combines in his work an affection for and a certain cynicism about his subjects that can be considered the basis of strong parody. By making painterly objects rather than paintings, Oldenburg was able to carry this direction further, while Peter Saul – a frequently expatriate Chicago painter whose style is also expressionist-derived (Gorky) – retains a de Kooningesque technique and acrid colour despite his subject matter: cartoon balloons, toilet seats, daggers, guns, dollar signs, and ubiquitous phallic protuberances. His intention is totally different from that of the hard-core Pop artists, though he was bracketed with them in the early days of the movement. For Saul really is a new humanist, as evidenced by his statements, and a broad satirist, as evidenced by his work. He has cited those 'strong facts' found in magazines and newspapers – the horrors and sensations that have such appeal for everyone today. In this he parallels Warhol's *Death and Disaster* series, depicting the dogs of Birmingham; automobiles, plane, or train wrecks; the tunafish catastrophe; electric chairs. Saul attempts to intensify the experience: 'These are not tender times. It seems very difficult to make anything happy convincing. But I am soft-hearted. I want to show that human beings are really okay.'[21]

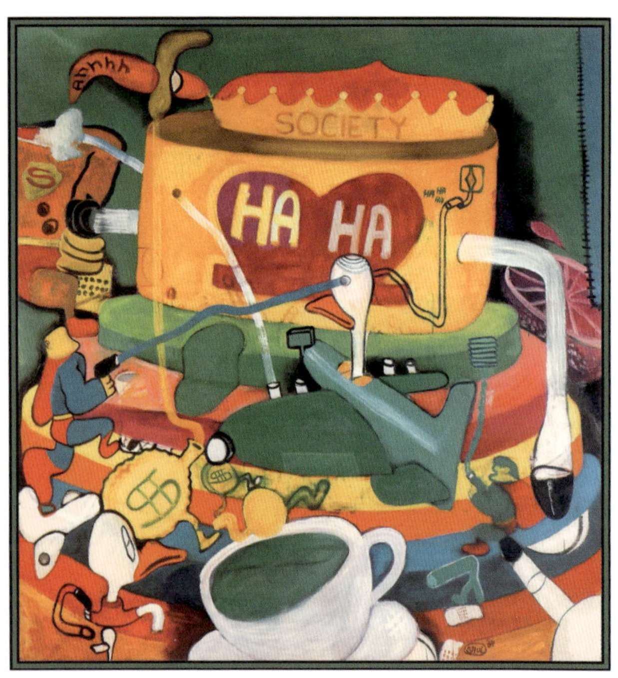

13. Peter Saul, *Society*, 1964. Oil on canvas

Warhol, on the other hand, refuses to comment, and aligns himself with the spectator who looks on the horrors of modern life as he would look at a TV film, without involvement, without more than slight irritation at the interruption by a commercial, or more than slight emotion at tear-jerking or calamitous events. In this respect Warhol is far more true than Saul to the attitudes of our technological society. Not everyone is so apathetic that he will watch a rape or murder without acting to prevent it, but many are. Most of us are unmoved by the public and private disasters that touched and enraged artists and thinkers in the 1930s. After World War II the tear glands of the world dried up from over-use. It is this world for which Warhol is spokesman; few can throw the first stone. Perhaps the reason the visual humanisms of the last decade have by and large failed so miserably with their horrified withdrawal, tormented expressionism, or mutilated-victim protest, is because their supposedly universal bases are not in fact shared by their audience. Since *everyone* understands the process of dehumanization blatantly and impersonally described by Warhol, his work is more likely to produce a positive attitude than the righteous indignation of those who are *against* anything in the present, and *for* nothing but a vague, outmoded nostalgia. As Warhol has pointed out, 'Those who talk about individuality most are the ones who most object to deviation, and in a few years it may be the other way around. Some day everybody will probably be thinking alike; that is what seems to be happening.' These ideas find parallels in those of the French painter Jean Dubuffet, who has said: 'My system rests on the identical character of all men.... If all painters signed their works with this one name: picture painted by Man, this question of differentiating, classifying, measuring men by various standards, would be meaningless.... What interests me is not cake, but bread,' and asserts his anti-cultural position by saying that his aim is to bring 'disparaged values into the limelight'.[22] Statements such as these provoked as much antagonism in the early 1950s as Warhol's do today, although the artistic results are poles apart.

While Warhol may be the most impersonal of the Pop artists, he too draws his subjects from his own experience – that second-hand experience which we all share. He has run the gamut of Pop subjects, with love and its commercialization and vulgarization a constant favourite. Warhol likes the idea that his life has dominated him. The *Death and Disaster* paintings, despite, or rather because of, their 'mechanical' execution, become one of the few forceful statements on this aspect of American life to be found in recent American painting. Just as we are fascinated by the newspaper or magazine photographs that are their sources, so we are doubly titillated by confronting these photographs in a less casual context – that of art – even if, as Warhol points out, 'when you see a gruesome picture over and over again, it doesn't really have any effect'. Rhetoric is no longer either necessary or significant; our senses are so overloaded with artificial emotion from politicians' speeches, bad movies, bad art, ladies' magazines, and TV soap operas that a *stark* repetition like Warhol's means more than an ultra-expressionist portrayal of accident victims ever could. Gesture is of prime importance in the new art. It is neither the physical gesture of the Expressionist nor the ironic gesture of Duchamp, but an unequivocal act that is both simple-minded and intellectually complex. Warhol's films and his art mean either nothing or a great deal. The choice is the viewer's, as it is with the plays of Beckett and Albee, the films of Antonioni, and the novels of Butor, Sarraute, or Robbe-Grillet. The more that is left out, the more can be seen of what is left. In Warhol's 'box show' at the Stable Gallery in 1964, which consisted of piles of wooden boxes simulating supermarket cartons with the brand insignias silkscreened on the sides (Brillo, Heinz, Del Monte, Campbell's), the idea was paramount, but became concrete only in visible form. Oldenburg, whose art is quite different from Warhol's, admired this show because it was 'a very clear statement, and I admire clear statements... . There's a degree of removal from actual boxes, and they become an object that is not really a box, so in a sense they are an illusion of a box and that places them in the realm of art'.

Whether or not Warhol is indifferent to his subjects does not affect our own responses. He is the most popular of the Pop artists; he did the cover for the 'teen-age' edition of *Time*, yet his *Most Wanted Men* were erased from the side of a New York World's Fair building as too controversial. Warhol is not by a long shot the best artist in conventional terms, but he is one of the most important artists working today, by virtue of his leadership of the uncompromisingly conceptual branch of abstract art.

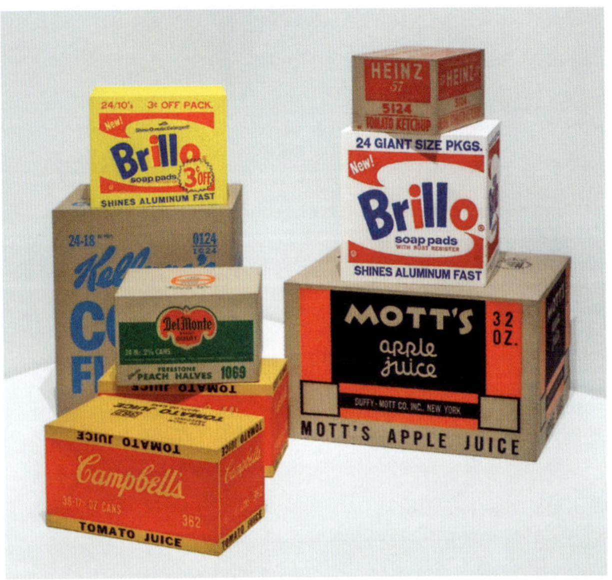

14. Andy Warhol, *Campbell's Tomato Juice Box*, *Del Monte Peach Halves Box*, *Heinz Tomato Ketchup Box*, *Kellog's Cornflakes Box*, *Mott's Apple Juice Box*, *White Brillo Box*, *Yellow Brillo Box*, 1964. Synthetic polymer paint and screenprint on wood

Two other artists initially associated with Pop Art, but devoted to satirical and 'human interest' values outside of it, are Marisol (Escobar) and George Segal. Marisol owes her techniques of painted wood sculpture to her original mentor – William King – although she has carried them into the area of Assemblage by adding extraneous objects and plaster casts, by working skilfully in and out of three dimensions, drawing, sculpting, and painting on her wood figures. Marisol rarely, if ever, uses commercial motifs, although her *John Wayne* and *The Kennedy Family* would fall within Pop iconography, and her wit is chic and topical.

Segal forgoes the toughness of Pop Art, and its humour too. His plaster moulds are made from the live model so that the true likeness is on the inside, and invisible. He has more in common with Allan Kaprow than with Pop; his *tableaux* of white figures in real-object environments (next to a Coke machine, in a bus driver's seat, against a cinema marquee) are like quick-frozen Happenings. While Segal's single or grouped figures can be extraordinarily evocative, their muteness stems less from detachment than from the distance imposed upon them by their ghostly hue. He is really a twentieth-century genre artist concerned with simple everyday activities that bring out a generalized humanity.

A second non-Pop vein, which specializes in social protest, should be mentioned, if only to dispel confusion by placing it properly outside Pop Art. That is the old March Gallery group, which got together around 1959 on Tenth Street and later moved uptown to the Gallery

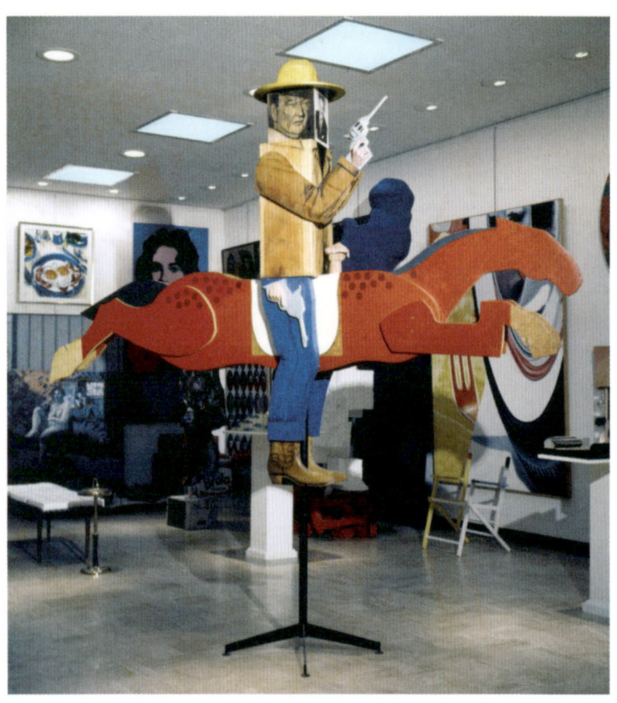

15. Marisol, *John Wayne*, 1963. Wood, mixed media

Gertrude Stein. Led by Boris Lurie, Sam Goodman and Stanley Fisher, these Assemblage, or 'Doom', artists are the political satirists that the Pop artists are not. They are all that Pop is not, and proclaimed themselves 'anti-Pop' in February 1964.[23] They are anguished, angry, and hot where Pop is cool, detached, and assured. They omit nothing from their conglomerations of trash, paint, collage, and objects, whereas the Pop artists omit almost everything from their direct presentation, and they are essentially pessimistic where Pop is optimistic. The March Gallery artists oppose the goals of the political cartoon to the goals of the advertisement. Their objects, designed to shock, are heavily dependent on ban-the-bomb horrenda – 'bloody' and dismembered dolls, crushed toys, primitive sexual fetishes, sado-masochistic *National Enquirer* photographs, girlie magazines. Belligerently romantic, as a group they come close to Neo-Dada. Their actual source is post-Abstract Expressionism – particularly Kaprow and Rauschenberg. They too are 'impatient with an art separated from life'.[24] Yet there is a febrile dispersiveness about Doom productions which fatally weakens them despite their devotion to admirable causes.

A third non-Pop parodistic current is represented by a single artist: Jim Dine. And although he is frequently included in the Pop rosters, his every work and statement show him to be worlds apart from that tough iconoclasm and formal emphasis. Dine is far closer to Johns, Rauschenberg, R. B. Kitaj, and the European Neo-Surrealists than to the Pop artists. The confusion with Pop probably began when he was one of the first

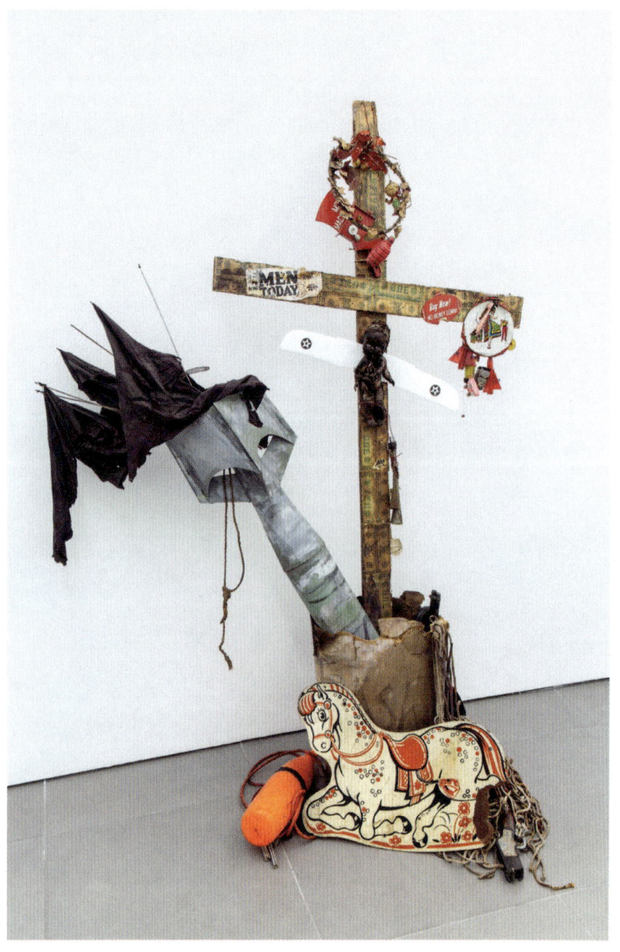

16. Sam Goodman, *The Bomb*, 1960–61. Found objects

to exhibit paintings of 'common objects' at the Martha Jackson Gallery early in 1962. His enormous ties, coats, hair or beads – labelled in an unambiguous non-Magrittean manner – were rendered in a technique and style unhealthily similar to that of Jasper Johns, although it has been noted that Johns in turn derived certain devices from Dine. By their 'giantism of popular imagery' and the fact that the objects were 'not scatalogical, but bought fresh', in Lawrence Alloway's words,[25] they were related to the work of Oldenburg, with whom Dine had been associated at the Judson and Reuben galleries, and, less so, to that of Rosenquist, Lichtenstein, and Warhol.

If Dine is not a Pop artist at all, why then, it might well be asked, is Claes Oldenburg considered one of the hardcore? Oldenburg was among the earliest to propound a Pop attitude, and to use 'pure' Pop motifs. As he wrote in 1961: 'I am for the art of red and white gasoline pumps and blinking biscuit signs...I am for Kool-Art, 7-Up Art, Pepsi Art, Sunkist Art, Dro-Bomb Art, Pamryl Art, San-O-Med Art, 39 cents Art and 9.99 Art.'[26] He has consistently used 'commercial' subject matter and his objects, unlike Dine's, are always For Sale. Oldenburg has made no attempt to disguise the Expressionist–Surrealist sources of his art because his powers of invention are strong enough to absorb them. In 1958 he was painting rather conservative nudes and portraits, but a year or so later his passionate involvement with the city provoked a more original art. His Judson Gallery exhibition in 1959, 'The Street', reflected the influences of Jean Dubuffet and the novelist Céline. But where Dubuffet's primitivism is a timeless one,

Oldenburg's referred specifically to the modernity and vulgarity of America: New York, Manhattan, the Lower East Side. Beginning with the grey, black and brown cardboard or *papiermâché* urban-refuse objects and the newspaper reliefs (such as *Céline Backwards*, 1960), grotesque figures (such as *Bride*, 1961), 'The Store' and its 'saleable' objects that blossomed out in bright primary coloured plaster in 1961 and grew to monstrous sizes in 1962, Oldenburg's attachment to materials was evident. He shares with Dubuffet the gift of discerning art in the lowest form of matter – dust, dirt, and garbage; his early objects bear comparison to Dubuffet's sculptural figures of glue, newspaper, steel wool, roots. Oldenburg also shares with Max Ernst the gift of endowing found or accidental shapes, materials, or textures with fantasy and form; he is 'fond of materials which take the quick, direct impress of life... also those materials which, like wire, seem to have a life of their own – socking you back when you sock them. I like to let the material play a large part in determining the form'.[27] This attitude makes him a kind of 'Pop automatist', and he is heir to other aspects of Surrealism as well.

Unlike most of the Surrealists, however, and unlike their successors in the 'messy' vein, for instance, Oldenburg is not dependent upon juxtaposition for effect. Like all the Pop artists he takes his objects whole and unadorned. But unlike most of them, he has never made the complete transition from rough to pristine handling. His surfaces until recently were expressionistically pitted, striped by drips, or gawky and awkward. Like Dubuffet he sees art as a 'celebration', and his plaster objects were inspired

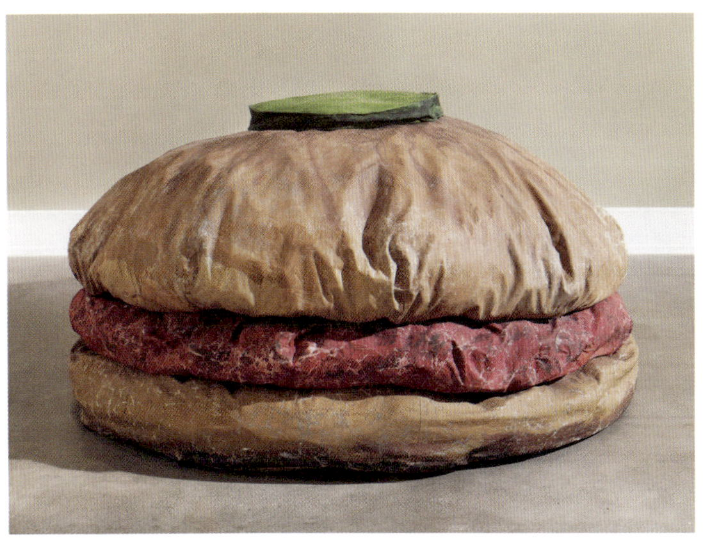

17. Claes Oldenburg, *Floor Burger*, 1962.
Canvas filled with foam rubber and cardboard boxes, painted with acrylic paint

by a desire to enhance life itself, in action: 'Painting, which has slept so long in its gold crypts, in its glass graves, is asked out to go for a swim, is given a cigarette, a bottle of beer, its hair rumpled, is given a shove and tripped, is taught to laugh... .'[28]

Finding paint too limiting for such freedom, Oldenburg went on to work with 'total space' in Happenings, then added plaster to his paint to make reliefs, and finally, free-standing objects. 'I'm not terribly interested in whether a thing is an ice-cream cone or a pie and so on... . The fact that I wanted to see something flying in the wind made me make a piece of cloth, the fact that I wanted to see something flow made me make an ice-cream cone.' He makes these things in order to 'give a concrete statement to my fantasy. Instead of painting it, to make it touchable, to translate the eyes into the fingers'. When Oldenburg uses actual ready-made objects, they are entirely integrated into the final 'scene' or environment – unlike those of Rauschenberg, Johns, Dine, or even Wesselmann. His 1961 *Stove*, for instance, is not 'transformed' as in Assemblage nor left to speak for itself as are ready-mades or found objects; it is recreated. Art and reality are unified, but each retains its own characteristics. This kind of interplay is at the heart of Oldenburg's creations. His cones and hamburgers, his bright pastries, vegetables, sandwiches, and meat are even appetizing at times; they are appealing because they combine gaiety with elephantine sadness. They are, as Apollinaire said of Picasso's objects, 'impregnated with humanity'. In this sense Oldenburg is a humanist, although it is a humanism

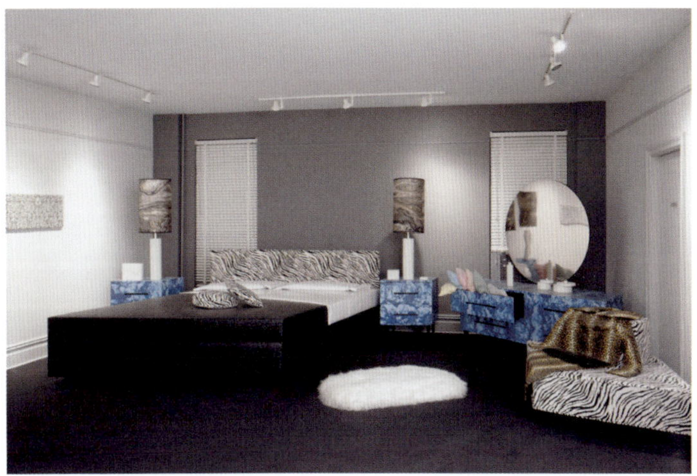

18. Claes Oldenburg, *Bedroom Ensemble,* 1963. Wood, vinyl, metal, artificial fur, cloth, and paper. The furniture is all rhomboidal. The sheets are shiny white vinyl, the bedspread quilted black plastic, the marbled accessories a strong, bilious turquoise; the 'paintings' on the walls are ordinary textile with a black embossed pattern like an imitation Jackson Pollock. The total effect is nightmarish.

devoid of sentimentality. Until 1965, his Pop Art was that of a sub-culture rather than a super-culture. It belonged to the shabby little stores and delicatessens on Second Avenue, the hopeful outdoor clothing racks of Orchard Street, the tawdry finery of Fourteenth Street, rather than the brand-new shiny department stores and ranch-style burger joints with ersatz wood panelling and chequered tablecloths.

With the furniture Oldenburg moved into the 'Home' period – a much more streamlined style that reflects Los Angeles, where it was executed and became fused with another sort of urbanity. In the luridly artificial grandeur of the *Bedroom*, shown in 1964 at Sidney Janis (a suite of furniture made 'in perspective' and nightmarishly glamourized with white vinyl sheets, textiles, mass-produced abstract paintings, and fake leopard-skin trimmings), or in the kinetic implications of *Ping-pong Table*, he began to extend 'cool' Pop imagery into new areas. His shiny vinyl 'soft objects' and their rough 'ghost' maquettes are among the most memorable Pop creations. Their shapes can be changed at touch, like Oyvind Fahlström's variable paintings, and they were conceived as 'new ways of pushing space around. 'If I didn't think what I was doing had something to do with enlarging the boundaries of art,' says Oldenburg, 'I wouldn't go on doing it'.

Tom Wesselmann's integration of objects into his paintings differs considerably from Oldenburg's, and from Dine's, Rauschenberg's, and the Assemblagists'. His one-wall interiors are not environments ('my rugs are not to be walked on'), nor are they paintings with decorative three-dimensional additions. They are, perhaps, a 'slice of life'. Wesselmann did not have to make a radical break with his previous style to become Pop. His small 'portrait collages' quite logically grew into the *Great American Nudes* for which he is best known. Fusing the arabesque and brilliant colour of Matisse with the sinuous line of Modigliani and a more rigorous framework traceable to Mondrian, the *Nudes* were first shown at the Tanager Gallery on Tenth Street in 1960. Unlike the rest of the artists discussed here, Wesselmann did not paint *from* magazine advertisements, billboards, and objects, but used them directly on the canvas, thus following conventional collage-assemblage methods. Only in 1964–65 did he finally abandon the real materials – and from necessity, for his work had become bigger and bigger, finally outgrowing its components. He first used ads from magazines, then from billboards; the objects grew apace, beginning with radios, fans, then windows, refrigerator doors, radiators. As his paintings enlarged, they tightened up: 'Colors became flatter, cleaner, brighter; edges became harder, clearer... . The sound of the paintings became sharper. I felt the need to lock up my paintings so tightly that nothing could move. This way, by becoming static and somewhat anonymous, they also became more charged with energy.'[29] This statement describes the experience of numerous young artists in the last five years – abstract as well as figurative.

During 1962–64 the *Great American Nudes* became bolder and more effective, incorporating ringing

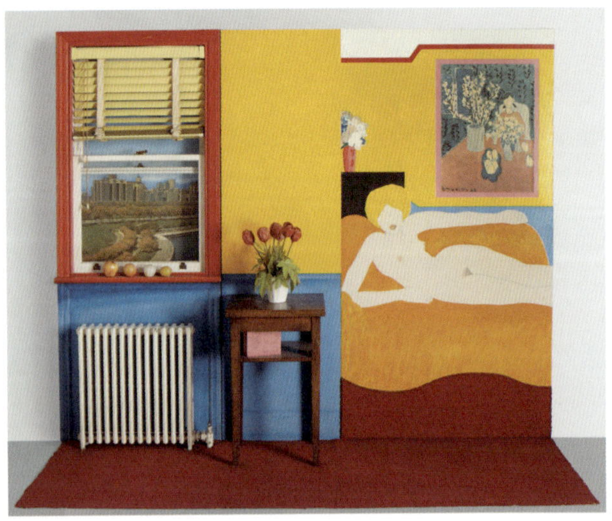

19. Tom Wesselmann, *Great American Nude No. 48*, 1963. Oil and collage on canvas, acrylic and collage on board, enamelled radiator and assemblage telephones, radios, and working TV sets. Changing constantly, the pictures were sentimental, satirical, nostalgic, or just plain silly, depending on whether *Lassie*, a political convention, an old movie, or an ad was on. In contrast with the shiny new furnishings or implements, the illusionistic collage pictures on the wall (George Washington, the *Mona Lisa*, Kennedy, Mickey Mouse), and views from the window, the nudes and painted backdrops were incongruously flat and stylized, often faceless or boldly patterned with stars and stripes. Wesselmann likes the 'reverberations' between painted and collage images, art history and advertising, *trompe-l'oeil* and reality. When he was forced to return to actual painting as the pieces got larger and collage materials scarcer, he discovered 'how audacious the act of painting is. One of the reasons I got started making collages was that I didn't have enough interest in a rose to paint it; I don't love roses or bottles or anything like that enough to sit down and paint them lovingly and patiently.... Now I had to invent a bowl and I couldn't believe how audacious it was'.

Paralleling the *Great American Nudes* was a series of less abstract still-lifes using similar elements, but more brand-name collage. Jill Johnston praised them in 1962 by saying, 'If a commercial advertising firm had a mind really to knock the public out for a hard sell, they might use one of Wesselmann's paintings'.[30] Some of them were as 'untransformed' as any Pop painting, although the masterful design and colour of the *Nudes* were perceptible behind the uncompromisingly unattractive array of products. Wesselmann's colour – brilliant and primary

– had always been one of the most interesting aspects of his work, and it took courage to abandon it and do a series of grisaille still-lifes in 1964–65. At first these incorporated real objects, or models of grey 'oranges' and labels recalling the paradoxical monotones of Johns, Watts, and Morris. Finally the constructions outgrew actual objects altogether. Only the landscapes – with almost life-size Volkswagen cut-outs – employed billboard materials. With them Wesselmann's work became belligerently simple, resembling that of Warhol and Lichtenstein more than his own previous production. Its 'modernization' parallels these artists' developments and Oldenburg's slick furniture. Wesselmann's immense blank beer cans, radios, bottles, fake façades of form resting on a shallow shelf are hollow, concave, or convex against stern rectilinear grounds. They have the clarity and strong design of the *Nudes* but lack the latter's *joie de vivre* and lively charm. At a moment when several of the other Pop artists are approaching a more aesthetic or abstract style, Wesselmann is moving away from one towards a pure commercial idiom.

Wesselmann's new austerity can be seen as part of the general purification of Pop Art. James Rosenquist, for example, says his images are 'expendable'. Yet once the choice is made, a stream-of-consciousness dialogue between images and artist ensues. 'Current methods in advertising, sublimation, and the hard sell, invade our privacy,' he has said. 'It's like getting hit with a hammer; you become numb. But the effect can be to move you into another reality. These techniques are annoying in the form in which they exist, but when they're used as tools by the painter, they can be more fantastic.'[31] Based on a painted collage concept of image juxtaposition, his painting bears a superficial resemblance to Surrealism; in intention it could not be more different. Rosenquist is not concerned with symbolism of any kind; his juxtaposed fragments do not act upon each other, but directly upon the spectator. The idea occurred to him while he was painting billboards for a living in New York in the late 1950s. His style was a sombre Abstract Expressionism at that time, but as he worked on the billboards, he began to realize that there was more potential innovation in his trade than in his art. He had become accustomed to seeing gigantic figures, objects, or seas of colour right up next to his face. As an abstract painter he was vitally attracted by the fact that such images close up lost all meaning or recognizability. Having gained through his billboard experience an insight into the spectacular possibilities of size (available to most of us only through the film), Rosenquist also sensed parallels with everyone's daily experience – especially in cities. He calls his work 'visual inflation. I'm living in it. Painting is probably more exciting than advertising – so why shouldn't it be done with that power and gusto, that impact?' In the winter of 1959–60 he made the breakthrough and discovered that he had escaped 'that old, pictorial space'.

Scale is the key to his work. The immense, sometimes unrecognizable images proceed from an inverse illusionism; they burst off the wall at the spectator in the initial encounter, but when the original impact has worn off, the skilful interlocking and subtle spatial devices holding them to the surface plane offer a rich visual experience to the viewer. The complex maelstrom of variously scaled images are knit into an intricate formal unity, every element firmly but unobtrusively related and held in the vice of the whole. Transparency, grisaille, relief panels, chromatic dislocation, subliminal suggestions, and above all an essentially abstract sensibility, are among the devices he uses. Once an ambiguous area in a Rosenquist painting is recognized as, say, a part of an umbrella, the linear pattern across it becomes rain. Each compartment does not contain an image, but the geometrical divisions conduct the orchestra of changes. A seven-foot leg, like that in *Over the Square,* throws the 'reality' of the entire canvas into question.

The climax of the compartmented style was the mural *F-111*, shown at the Castelli Gallery in April 1965. Eighty-six feet long and ten feet high, its theme is the position of the artist in an era of immensity, jet war machines, and *nouveaux collectionneurs*. It has been billed as 'the world's largest Pop painting', which hardly does it justice. The eye is rushed along the wall by the image of a jet bomber, stopping only for four weighty verticals that punctuate the horizontal movement of dazzling colour and aluminium.[32] The stamp of the man-made is ubiquitous in this as in all of Rosenquist's work. He wants to get 'as far away from nature as possible', and he is troubled by what he feels is a 'heavy hand of nature on the artist'. Figure or landscape references are often read into Abstract Expressionism, and the Pop artists, by leaving no question as to the origins of their images, seek to avoid these associations. By leaving the question of identity clear, they are free to make their own paintings, on their own terms, and these paintings often, conversely, appear to be abstract. In a painting and a construction entitled *Capillary Action I* and *II*, he depicted landscape elements with neon, plastic, and other unlikely elements, but included a real sapling tree, disrupting the common conceptions of nature and art, artifice and reality.

It is difficult to summarize the work of any of these artists in so little space, but with Rosenquist the difficulty is compounded. His is a complex, multiple art. Each painting demands detailed analysis of both its formal and emotional effects, and over the last five years he has encompassed a greater variety of techniques and materials than any of the other Pop artists. While the immense compartmented images (there may be two or twenty such fragments in a painting) remain the scaffolding of his experiments, he has set himself no other limitations. Since 1962 Rosenquist has employed extraneous materials such as diaphanous plastic sheets, mirror, Plexiglas, neon and electric light, paint-smeared or rainbow-spattered bits of wood or twine. Free-standing constructions, shaped canvases, hinged or pierced surfaces, new industrial and commercial materials – all have been part of his vocabulary for years. Rosenquist's free-wheeling inventiveness makes other Pop artists (except perhaps Oldenburg) look conservative, yet he has been called the academic of the group because of his quasi-photographic style of rendering images and his inverse illusionism. What he does with these techniques, however, is more important. By refusing to accept any limitations, often by abandoning fresh ideas before barely scratching their surfaces, Rosenquist continually demands more of himself and his art. He belongs to the romantic tradition.

Robert Indiana (*né* Robert Clark, in Indiana) has from the beginning straddled the gap between Pop iconography and abstraction. I have not included him in the hard-core because his work has always been fundamentally non-objective. On the other hand, he is perhaps the most 'literary' of all, and his attitudes have been as much in key with the Pop programme as anyone's. He was one of the first to exploit the new subject matter in his geometric abstractions derived from pinball machines and traffic signs; his colour and heraldic style can be traced to Ellsworth Kelly. Now that the trend of Pop Art is to the abstract, Indiana could be reinstated, although formally he is less of an innovator than the five men discussed here. His contribution has been the marriage of poetry and geometric clarity via the inclusion of American literature and history in a non-objective art. Despite his superficially 'purist' style, Indiana is an out-and-out romantic. His poetic invocations of Melville and Whitman and his references to Americana and specifically to the history of the lower Manhattan shipbuilding district are subordinated to the concentric rings of colour in which they are stencilled; once they are read, the canvas is transformed, the rings become wheels instead of pure form, and the

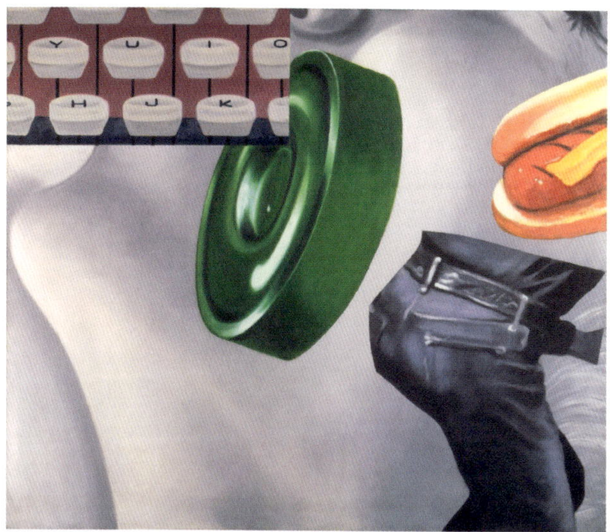

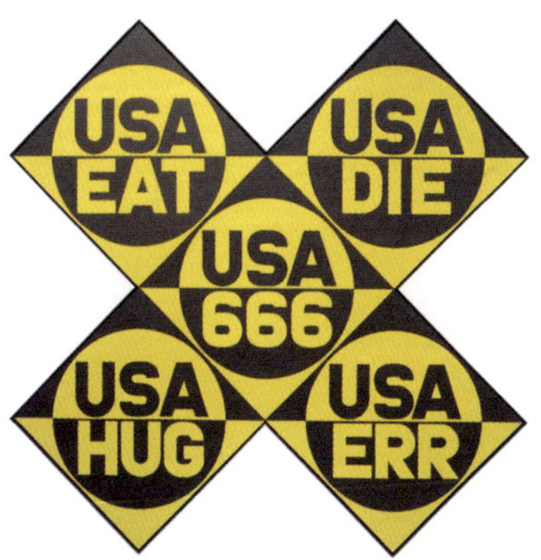

20. James Rosenquist, *The Lines Were Deeply Etched on the Map of Her Face*, 1962. Oil on canvas
21. Robert Indiana, *USA 666 (The Sixth American Dream)*, 1964–66. Oil on canvas. Indiana's *leitmotif* is the two sides of the American dream: one, the literature and history of America, the other, its way of life.

literary content surges to the surface. If the stencilled legends are not read, the paintings remain non-objective. In Indiana's *EAT* and *DIE* pieces or the highway route signs, the message is mistakable, though the format is still more cool and generalized, and the American Dream of easy life and death is pointedly the subject. In this manner he is also able to inject more than the usual amount of outright social comment into his work, though he does so only occasionally, as in the Selma, Alabama painting ('Just as in the anatomy of man, every nation must have its hind part'), or by single-word references of a topical nature. Roy Lichtenstein has been most closely associated with the 'new' or 'cool' abstraction – surprising, perhaps, since his work was for years the most conspicuously narrative and representational. In a sense, his paintings have the opposite effect from Indiana's; they become *less* rather than more literary with perusal. The insistent dramas of love and war interest Lichtenstein less than 'the formal problem... . Once I've established what the subject matter is going to be, I'm not interested in that... . I think of it as abstract painting when I do it. Half the time they're upside-down anyway when I work'. Most Pop Art is essentially emblematic in its conjunction of word and image. Lichtenstein shares with 'post-painterly abstraction' his enlarged scale, broad flat forms on colour fields, carefully depersonalized line, reductive composition, and expanded forms that seem to exist beyond the framing edge. Some earlier paintings had been virtually non-objective, even when specific objects were depicted; the *Explosions* are dynamic, spiky forms that have been lifted from their grounds and made into star-like reliefs of uncompromising vulgarity. *Golf Ball*, 1962, is a single sphere with patterned, variously directional semi-circular grooves; *Magnifying Glass* has a dazzling field of Ben Day dots, enlarged in the centre; and *Before and After* – two holes in rectangular patches of fabric – utilizes abstract and optical conventions. These were also much in evidence in the double-surfaced landscapes, where a slightly off-register optical vibration occurs when a dotted sheet of clear Plexiglas is laid over another surface, or Ben Day screens (previously employed to reproduce dots) are superimposed on each other.

During 1964, Lichtenstein's work became increasingly abstract as the comic images moved closer and closer to the spectator; for subject matter he turned to Greek temples, and to landscapes – sunsets, sunrises, seas, and cloudy skies – once removed from reality like the comic strips, since they refer to travel posters and dime-store art. After being reduced to striking three-colour rectangles divided by a horizon line or an Art Nouveau whiplash, these became reliefs of plastic or enamel on metal. The logical outcome was the 'sculpture' begun in 1965: precariously stacked cups and saucers, pitchers, heads of comic-strip characters made with the aid of a professional ceramist. Witty and fresh, these are the first sculptures about painting, for each object is treated as though it were two-dimensional, with all the flattening devices of Lichtenstein's paintings – half-tone screening, bright solid colour shadows, heavy outlines, and metallic highlights.

By the exhibition season of 1962–63 Pop Art was already attracting new adherents, only a few of whom had valid contributions to make before a third wave appeared. The second wave included artists who were working towards a Pop style by 1961 and others who were influenced but not overwhelmed by the hard core. Among the former was John Wesley, who had come from California to New York in 1960 and showed at the Robert Elkon Gallery in 1962. Wesley's whimsical emblems, enshrined in floral or decorative borders and painted in a deceptively sweet poster style, celebrate old-fashioned sports figures, ladies' lacrosse teams, squirrels and presidents, often in pale blue and white with pink-and-green touches and black outlines. In 1965 he made some furniture decorated with zany figures – pregnant women and bearded men on bicycles. The strength of Wesley's work derives from its apparent innocence, even coyness, fused with an underlying eroticism. His wit is a curious one – partially subtle and Surrealist (the juxtapositions of cows and dancing nudes, baseball players and garlands), but also broadly humorous in the sight-gag tradition. Although reflecting commercial imagery less than a family-album folk art, the paintings are executed in a no-nonsense hard-edge style.

Allan D'Arcangelo showed at the Fischbach Gallery in 1962 and there preempted an ultra-Pop subject matter for his own: the American highway speeding vertiginously into the future – a knife-edged path punctuated by billboards, route and speed-limit signs, and an occasional languid female hitchhiker. The distance leaps toward the

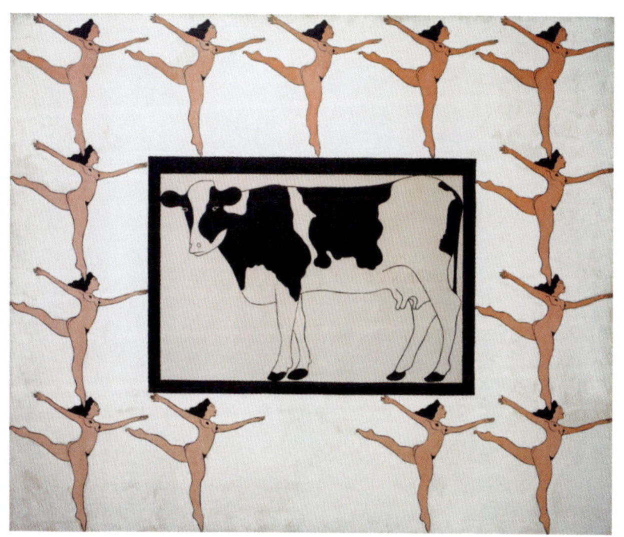

22. John Wesley, *Holstein*, 1964. Oil on canvas

viewer and accentuates the velocity. By employing the conventions of non-objective hard-edge art, silhouetted forms and a restricted but brilliant palette, D'Arcangelo often achieves a striking simplicity that firmly allies him with the hard-core Pop artists.

Marjorie Strider's bathing beauties made their début at the Pace Gallery's First International Girlie Show in 1963. They stood out, literally, with protruding buttocks, lips, and breasts carved from wood and later from the lighter styrofoam, which enabled her to build larger, gravity-defying sections. Half painted, half sculpted, rendered in a crude commercial idiom like that of Lichtenstein, these figures are conceived in resolutely formal terms, more apparent when the pin-ups gave way to immense flowers and vegetables in 1964, and in 1965 to great free-standing or hanging sculptures of landscape elements (clouds, moon, beach) with the rectilinear outlines of a window frame painted on them.

Robert Watts, one of the more eccentric artists to be connected with Pop Art, predicted as well as participated in its inception. His postage-stamp machine, dispensing distinctly non-governmental issue, was a memorable creation. Like the Duchamp- and Johns-derived object artists, Watts deals in paradox, exposing the nature of perception and deception in his common objects. The 'heavy foodstuffs', made of gleaming chrome-plated lead, the rows of graded white, grey, and black loaves of bread, the transparent sandwiches or fake-fur popsicles parallel Oldenburg's subject matter but relinquish the robust qualities in favour of attractiveness.

Alex Hay's cut-out utilities, Leo Jensen's good-natured heroes, Vern Blosum's telephones, Don Nice's fruit ads, Milet Andrejevic's stylized US mailboxes on raw canvas, Steve Antonakos' stencilled Dream pillowcases, Aaron Kuriloff's unadorned utilities, Robert Moscowitz's window shades, and certain of Robert Whitman's uncategorizable film-environment object creations are also legitimately related to Pop of the early period. Rosalyn Drexler's photograph-derived celebrities, love scenes, and dramatic news shots have the immediacy and colour but not the technique associated with Pop. Like Idelle Weber's mute urban groups moving across chequerboard grounds, and Harold Stevenson's monstrous enlargements of the male anatomy, they are motivated by different attitudes. There are several well-known artists who do not subscribe to the Pop impersonalism, but react to contemporary phenomena with a similar excitement. To this extra-Pop area can be assigned Richard Lindner's increasingly brutalized banners and recent paintings in which the Léger-Beckmann figures sport teen-age gang jackets, bat-winged sunglasses, and garish colour to augment the repressed violence of his personal style, isolated plasters by Peter Agostini (the clothes line, the carousel), Yayoi Kusama's phallus-studded furniture, Red Grooms' movie-star and movie-set cutouts, Alex Katz's Revolutionary War soldiers (designed in 1961 as stage sets), Ernest Trova's *Falling Man* series. In addition, there is the third string of Pop artists, largely repetitious and inept, of interest mainly because they prove that Pop Art, like any other art, cannot be necessarily done by anyone so inclined.

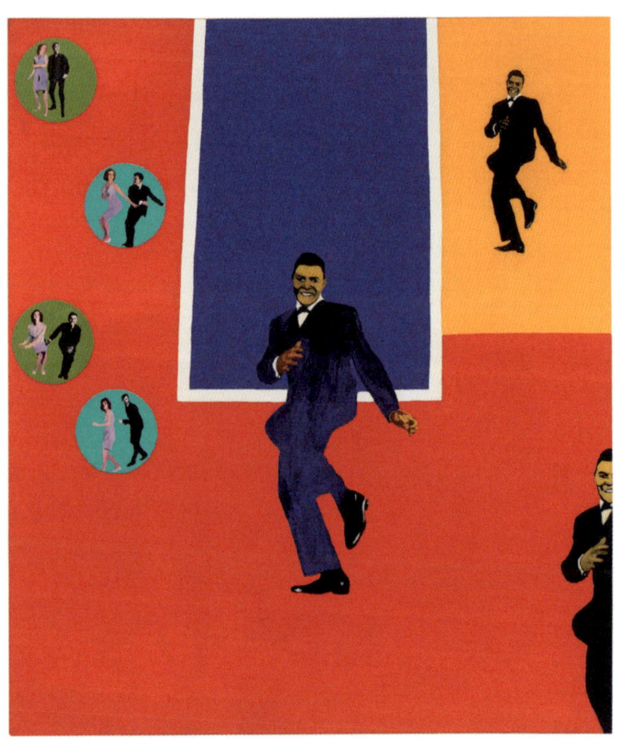

23. Rosalyn Drexler, *Chubby Checker*, 1964.
Acrylic, oil, paper collage on canvas

Merely choosing a jazzy commercial image to concentrate on is not enough. Among them there is a drift toward simple, often tasteless jokes or bold pornography as subject matter, and their styles often depart from hard-edge Pop to return to a more generalized Assemblage mode. The force of the original group becomes even more apparent when viewed in the light of its imitators.

Forcing a change of attitude toward 'art', 'art materials', and 'art-worthy subjects', the original Pop artists, like all innovators before them, have altered the way in which we see the world. Others have been affected who could not by the wildest stretch of the imagination be called Pop. Andy Warhol's new conceptions of mass production, the anti-sculptural structures of Donald Judd and Robert Morris, the paintings of Frank Stella and Larry Poons – whose work, like Pop, has seemed to many people too sparse to be art – have spawned what Max Kozloff has called 'dissimulated Pop':[33] the handsome boxy furniture of Richard Artschwager, Irwin Fleminger's 1964 *Subway Unit* (in which formica I-beams, a white 'scale', an orange-and-blue 'trash can' and plastic 'gum machines' referred to these common objects in a general rather than a descriptive manner), or Robert Smithson's 1965 panels of metal-flecked plastic, as vulgar as Hollywood Modern bar sculpture. Robert Mangold's non-objective paintings were initially suggested by the lettering on truck sides, and his *Walls* by prefabricated buildings.

Industrial materials like Formica, chrome, Day-Glo and aluminium paints, false wood-grain or wallpaper textures, cheap textiles, plastics, automobile enamels, lacquers, and neon light have added to the formal possibilities of the new art. Rosenquist's shaped canvases, commercial paints, and 'invented materials' (like chrome-plated barbed wire), Lichtenstein's enamel editions of his paintings, Warhol's box show and helium-filled silver pillows all have had repercussions. Oldenburg's work has been particularly influential, above all his *Bedroom*. His vinyl and kapok objects, or 'soft sculpture', have signalled a fertile direction; several highly individual artists (who may or may not consider Oldenburg a direct source) work with cloth or similar materials as an abstract sculptural medium, fusing aspects of Pop, Surrealism, and non-objective art: Frank Lincoln Viner, Eva Hesse, Alice Adams, Jean Linder, Anne Wilson, and Marc Morrell. Chryssa, Dan Flavin, and Steve Antonakos use neon or fluorescent light and others are using a non-art palette of insipid ice-cream shades or 'kandy kolors', glow-in-the-dark tones, Howard Johnson's or institutional decorators' hues like turquoise, pistachio, mauve, lavender, and peach – hitherto considered too bland for fine art, unless employed sparingly in delicate touches.[34]

The popularity of eye-catching target and stripe motifs, bold patterning, zigzag shapes and hard outlines, a certain flashy crudity of presentation, a disregard for 'composition' and strictly aesthetic enjoyment – all the main characteristics of a 'difficult art' that refuses decorative security – are part of the same phenomenon that produced Pop.

EUROPE AND CANADA

THE FURTHER IN SPIRIT the cultural heritage of a country is from that of America, the more tenuous is the bond between Pop Art and related manifestations in that country. There is no hard-core Pop Art in Europe, although there are a few artists in Germany, Italy, and France who approach either its subject matter or its techniques. This is true for a number of reasons, one of the simplest being that a different tradition and living conditions produce a different art.

Pop Art in particular seems to be the product of an affluent society. It is also produced by and consequently directed at the postwar generation – artists who were growing up during the Second World War. One need only compare the childhoods of a Frenchman, an Italian, a German, an Englishman, and an American who grew up between 1938 and 1945 to understand the fundamental differences in their art. This also explains why Germany, which with its ultra-modern industrial society would seem an ideal breeding ground, has produced little Pop Art. For everyone but the Americans, Americanization has an exotic appeal. It may be despised, romanticized, glamourized, idealized, but it is rarely taken for granted. By emphasizing the picturesque, the ominous, the satirical aspects of commercial subject matter, the Europeans are being true to themselves. To create a genuine Pop Art, a European artist would have to disentangle the Pop motifs of Americanization from his own heritage; a clean break is usually impossible as well as undesirable.

The European urban arts are called 'new realism', a term most Americans or English would forgo because of its philosophical implications. Pierre Restany's group, christened the Nouveaux Réalistes on 16 April 1960 in his first manifesto (written on the occasion of an exhibition at the Galleria Apollinaire in Milan), is by far the most important and seminal of these. For most of the artists associated with Restany, the transposition of a single commercial image or object on to canvas without apparent alteration would be unthinkable; it would be too simple, too lacking in intellectual challenge.

Restany's initial distaste for the work of Warhol and Lichtenstein was expressed in his article on the Sidney Janis Gallery's 'New Realists' exhibition in New York in 1962. He doubted that these two painters would still be talked about in two years, and found that the 'platitude of tones and dry rigour of commercial painting' left the spectator undernourished; he ended by congratulating Janis for bringing to New York this 'revivifying breath from Europe'. Actually, although the title of the show had been borrowed from Restany, the European contributions looked pale, overworked, and strongly Surrealizing compared with the new Pop Art. For the Nouveaux Réalistes are primarily Assemblagists, and there was already a plethora of Assemblage being shown in New York – some better, some worse. Since 1962, critics and museums all over the world have sought to confuse the various New Realisms and Pop Art, but it is clear by now that they should be viewed as two totally separate visual phenomena.

There are, however, significant similarities in the impetus behind both the European and the Anglo-American trends. The return to a New Realism of any kind was born of discontent with the further possibilities of an abstract, spontaneous art. Neither the New Realists nor the Pop artists were interested in the 'new figurations' that stemmed from Francis Bacon or Goya. Both were far more involved with the ordinary artifacts of an industrial and luxury-oriented civilization. Yet the Americans take their daily reality straight, whereas the Europeans are likely to call their sources 'daily mythologies'.[35] Stylistically and formally, the European artist is not as aggressive as the American, but he is given to manifestoes and demonstrations that are ferocious, emotional, and *engagé* in contrast to the 'cool' Anglo-American viewpoint, which spurns group identification. The Parisian attitude toward the New Reality is far more literary. Restany promulgates a sociological point of view toward art that holds little interest for Pop artists, although it has provided their critics with food for thought. The American group that had most in common with the New Realists, and corresponded chronologically as well, is Allan Kaprow's circle and other proto-Pop figures such as Edward Kienholz on the West Coast or Peter Blake in England. The writings of the New Realists include references to such New York School phrases as the act, the gesture, throwaway and expendable materials. Restany himself has found similarities between his protégés and Rauschenberg or Johns, once comparing César's crushed and compressed automobiles to John Chamberlain's sculpture; actually, their differences and those between most of their respective colleagues are only stressed by such a comparison. César's cars are acts of defiance; Chamberlain merely picked a colourful and available raw material with which to make abstract sculpture. A major factor in the divergence between European and American developments, which began so close but matured so differently, is that the non-relational trend gathering strength in America at the time had no counterpart in Europe.

The first Nouveau Réalisme exhibition, in Milan, included Yves Klein, Tinguely, Hains, Villeglé, Dufrêne, and Arman, but officially the group was formed some months later in Paris, on 27 October 1960. César and the Italian Mimmo Rotella also participated in the early group activities, and later Niki de Saint Phalle, Deschamps, and Christo joined the ranks. In May 1961, they held their first Paris exhibition – '40° au-dessus de Dada' (40 degrees above Dada) at Restany's Galerie J. The title of this show is significant, for the New Realists had made no attempt to break with the strong Dada and Surrealist tradition still existing in Paris. On the contrary, by pointing to Duchamp's ready-mades as their source, they proudly proclaimed their legitimacy, and it is impossible to overemphasize Duchamp's influence on their activities. While a certain blatant iconoclasm and wit allied them to Dada rather than to Surrealism, Surrealism is the obvious predecessor of many New Realist objects, and its trenchant eroticism is another major legacy. The New Realists rarely let the chosen object speak for itself, as Duchamp's ready-mades or Johns' ale cans did, but invest it with a soupçon of mystery and elegance by fragmentation, juxtaposition, or slight alteration. It is not the directness, the banality, the refreshing anonymity of urban reality that appeals to them, but the hitherto unrecognized strangeness latent in every common object, old or new.

Yves Klein, who died in 1962 at the age of thirty-four, was the most influential member of the New Realists. He had virtually nothing to do with Pop Art, but is so important to the entire French *avant-garde* that he must be mentioned here. 'Yves le monochrome', as he called himself, has become something of a legend. In the 1940s he began to work with solid-colour canvases, finally settling on royal blue for most of his work. In April 1958 he produced an exhibition at the Iris Clert gallery in Paris which consisted of an empty room. Because of his extraordinary flair for theorizing the spiritual *tabula rasa*, Klein corresponds in importance to John Cage in America. Otto Hahn has pointed out that Klein's 'colour was given not as the transcription of an emotion but as reality'.[36] The closest Klein came to figuration was his 'body prints', made by manipulating nude models covered in blue paint against white canvases. But he considered all of his efforts – monochrome, air, the fire and water pieces – as realism, saying: 'I am the painter of space. I am not an abstract painter, but representational and realistic.'[37] Klein's activities indicate the breadth of New Realism in comparison to Pop Art, and Klein at least, no matter how pretentiously, humorously or profoundly he went about it, did go at least forty degrees beyond Dada.

Most of the New Realists have not gone so far. By transforming the function, and often the appearance, of an object, they create a subjective rather than an objective reality. Martial Raysse is the only member of the original group to share both image and techniques with the Anglo-American Pop artists, although his style is still lyrical, his approach more intellectual and satirical than theirs. Raysse's *Beach*, 1962, was a *tableau* rather like those of Edward Kienholz, but since then he has moved from dime-store assemblage to Pop painting with experimental touches such as movies projected on the canvas, neon detail, and images photographically reproduced on the canvas. Raysse's art is based on a peculiarly ultramodern sense of beauty and ugliness; he has made a series of *tableaux affreux* (frightful pictures), and another of 'Made in Japan' pictures which 'improve upon' old-master paintings with lurid colours and patterns. His neon-accented landscapes go nature one better and 'compete with life'. Raysse is from Nice, and his favourite image is appropriately the bathing beauty, preferably sunglassed, and tanned a garish orange or pink tint (if not green). An exuberant jet-set eroticism and comic possibility pervades all of his work. Related to Raysse in the use of old masters as models for vulgar, photographic paintings in acrid colours is the relative newcomer to the New Realists – Alain Jacquet.

Some of the New Realists have so little relation to Pop that they will not be treated here. Tinguely is a kinetic

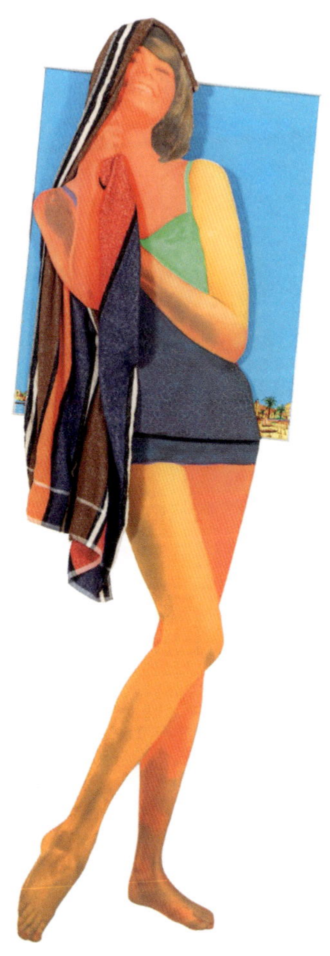

24. Martial Raysse, *Baigneuse sur quatre plans*, 1963.
Acrylic on canvas, photography and collage on panel, towel

sculptor, César an abstract sculptor, Niki de Saint Phalle a compelling religious fetishist and mythologian, though maybe her shooting at her plaster and toy assemblages with a rifle was a 'realist' gesture in Restany's sense. Outside of the New Realist fold, but similarly inclined, are artists like Daniel Pommerville, who has made a variety of paintings and object paintings based on a clothes-hanger motif and simple objects like a neat coil of barbed wire, a chair with a plastic shopping bag hung from it. Erik Dietmann neatly covers common objects and furniture with strips of 'bandage' – an obsession paralleling that of Yayoi Kusama who, although she works in New York, is closer to the Surrealist approach of the Parisians. Roy Adzak makes pale relief moulds of objects; Tetsumi Kudo makes glass and plastic 'surgical' constructions; Philippe Hiquily has made a stylized iron figure that rides a real motorcycle; Jean-Pierre Raynaud does geometric sign paintings, Edmund Alleyn paints abstract machines, and Monory, Gilli, and Pavlos share a quasi-New Realist attitude.

Few of those listed above are wholly or even peripherally devoted to the New Realist programme. Armand Fernandez Arman, however, is a Nouveau Réaliste *par excellence*. His all-over accumulations, which have their roots in some rubber-stamp drawings made in 1954 under the influence of Jackson Pollock, exist in limbo between abstraction and figuration. His collections of ball-bearings have a direct precedent in a Surrealist object by Man Ray, and Arman is frank about the fact that he is not doing anything new, but only 'bringing a little facet of reality through the prism of all the arts of all times'.[38]

By accumulating groups of identical or similar objects in a glass case, Arman seeks to 'suspend events, stop speed or explosion'. The same thing is accomplished by his *colères* (tantrums), which are 'action sculptures' – objects smashed, crushed, or otherwise destroyed and then mounted, often in decorative patterns; and his *coupes* (cross-sections) – objects sliced into silhouetted reliefs.

Christo (born Christo Javacheff in Bulgaria) has also carried an idea originated by Man Ray to new extremes. The latter's *Enigma of Isidore Ducasse* presented a mysteriously wrapped shape; from this Christo has developed an obsession with packaging, as a modern industrial technique rather than a theatrical guessing game. Over the last few years he has packaged everything from people to bicycles. Recognizable or unrecognizable, tightly, even sadistically bound, his lumpy parcels have a distinctive ambiguity as well as evoking a natural curiosity about their contents. Christo expanded into life-size store fronts with veiled windows draped by clear plastic. In June, 1962, he filled the Rue Visconti in Paris with an accumulation of oil cans (*Rideau de fer*), an act paralleled by Allan Kaprow's environment at Martha Jackson's in New York, 1961 – a backyard filled with automobile tyres.

Öyvind Fahlström, who was born in Brazil, spans the gap between Anglo-American and New Realist attitudes. While he uses Pop images taken from magazine illustrations and comics, and began with intricately detailed 'abstract comic-strips' in the early 1960s, his art is concerned with far more complex ends. In the 'variable paintings' the figures and images can be moved to form

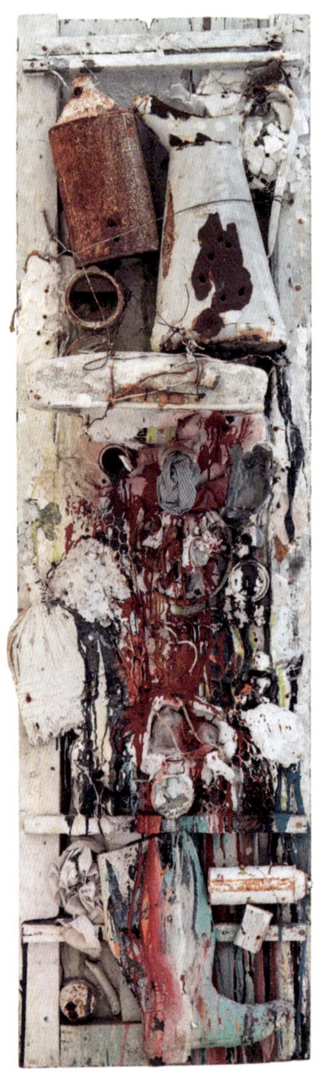

25. Niki de Saint Phalle, *Homage to Bob Rauschenberg (shot at by Rauschenberg)*, 1961. Paint, plaster, various objects on a wooden shutter

26. Arman, *Bebida Loca*, 1960. Accumulation of capsules of soda bottles in wooden box, Plexiglas

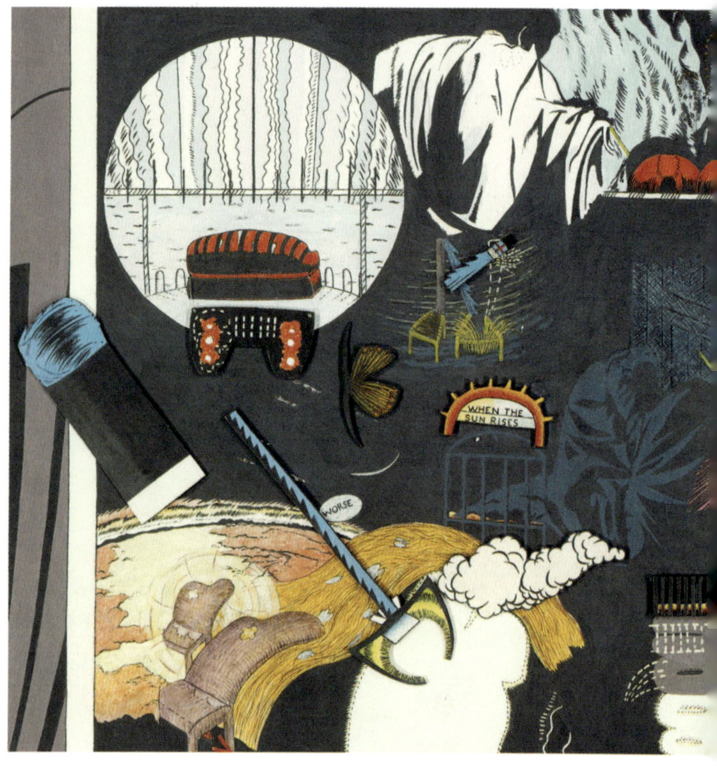

27. Öyvind Fahlström, *Sitting... Six months later*, 1963. Variable painting. Oil, gouache and collage with magnets, nylon threads, beads, wire and composition on canvas mounted on metal. In the 'variable paintings', image elements can be moved around on the surface to form new configurations.

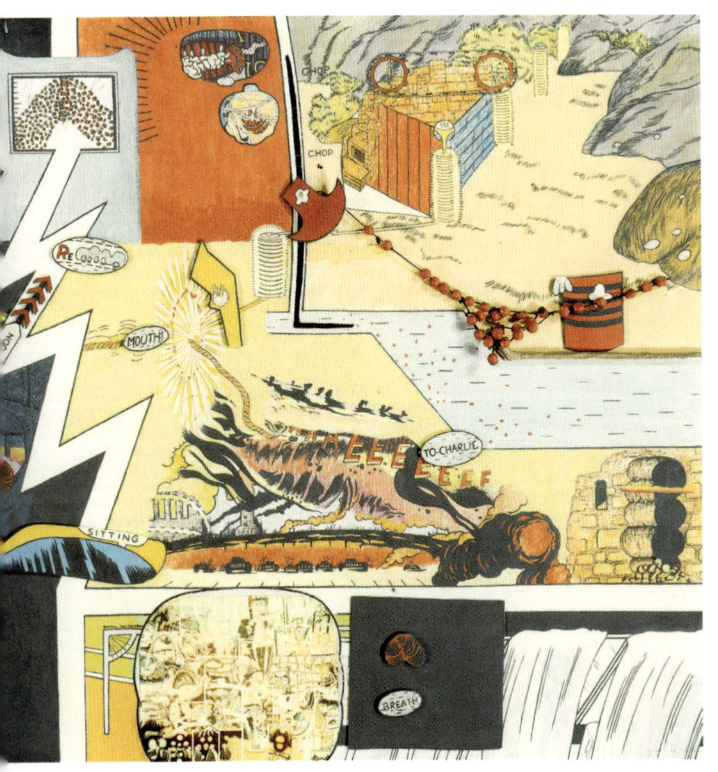
CHOP
CHOP
MOUTH!
TO CHARLIE
SITTING
BREATH

any number of different pictures. They are manipulated on hinges or by magnets, as in *Planetarium*, which is fundamentally a paper-doll game – the figures can be dressed and their 'characters' changed. Fahlström explained his idea in an essay, 'A Game of Character': 'A game structure means neither the one-sidedness of realism, nor the formalism of abstract art, nor the symbolic relationship in surrealistic pictures, nor the balanced unrelationship in "neo-dadaist" works. The arrangement grows out of a combination of the rules (the chance factor) and my intentions, and is shown in a "score" or "scenario" (in the form of a drawing, photographs, or small paintings). The isolated elements are thus not paintings, but machinery to make paintings. Picture-organ.'[39]

Paralleling Tinguely's meta-matic sculptures, which may draw pictures or destroy themselves, Fahlström's paintings progress in time rather than in space (although the actual space in which his pictures operate is also a particularly disturbing one – discontinuous and fluctuating). Rauschenberg has written of the variable works: 'The logical or illogical relationship between one thing and another is no longer a gratifying subject to the artist as the awareness grows that even in his most devastating or heroic moment he is part of the density of an uncensored continuum that neither begins with nor ends with any decision or action of his.'[40]

Daniel Spoerri, a highly imaginative theorist, has carried Pop Art's implications much further than the Americans, though his work lags far behind his theories. He is best known for his 'snare pictures', in which objects arranged by chance (such as a table top complete with dirty glasses, ashes in the ashtray) are fixed and then hung on the wall. This is an extension of the ready-made or found-object principle; only the plane is altered (as it was in Rauschenberg's *Bed*), but any alteration at all opens the objects to new interpretation. Departing from Duchamp, Spoerri has made a close study of the laws of chance, according to which all reality operates. His American counterparts would be Kaprow or Cage. In October 1961, Spoerri paralleled Oldenburg's contemporary *The Store* with a *Grocery Shop* in the Galerie Köpke, Copenhagen. Ordinary perishable items (not made by the artist as were Oldenburg's) were 'chosen' as works of art, and so labelled. 'Does a tomato cease to be a tomato merely because it is named a work of art?' demands Spoerri. 'To buy a tomato while realizing that it's a work of art that one is buying is participating in a great spectacle. In a spectacle what is false becomes true, provided one enters into the game.'[41] Where Oldenburg's *Store* was a tangible gesture intended as an act of creation, Spoerri's was an intellectual game; both far outreach the purely commercial motifs of the Bianchini Gallery's *Supermarket*, in New York, 1964.

Among Spoerri's other manifestations were the June 1961 *Trunk*, in Cologne (where the spectators packed and unpacked the contents), and his *Anecdotal Topographies* at the Galerie Lawrence, Paris, 1962 (where objects were spread at random on a table and indicated on a chart with appropriate anecdotes). In New York, in 1964, Spoerri gave a dinner party for critics and artists and fixed the leftovers of each place-setting with epoxy for a

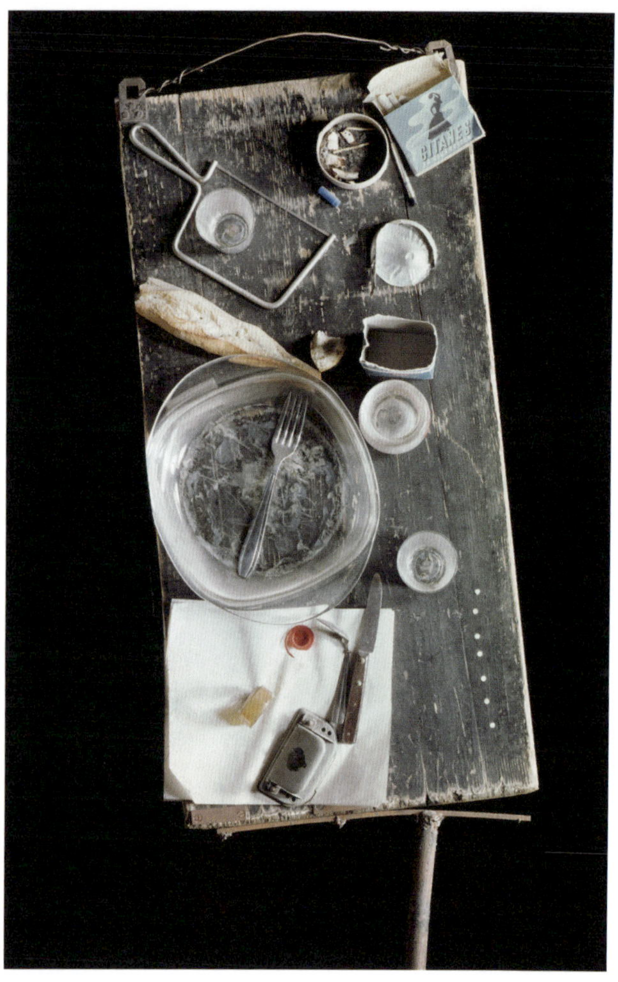

28. Daniel Spoerri, *Ci-gît Jean Onnertz, tableau-piège* (recto), 1960. Two-sided assemblage, objects and enamel signs on wooden board snare-picture exhibition at the Allan Stone Gallery; in 1965 he showed some 'collections' (groups of like objects reflected, repeated in different colours, photographed or real) in his crowded room at the Chelsea Hotel in New York under the auspices of the Green Gallery; Allan Kaprow wrote the catalogue preface.

Spoerri's events, like the early American Happenings, are more typical of the European *avant-garde* than of Pop Art. The Parisians, and the Germans, are greatly given to demonstrations of one sort or another. Some of them are conducted with an abandonment worthy of the Dada soirées. The artists involved do not have enough in common with Pop Art to be discussed here, although Jean-Jacques Lebel and the Icelander Ferrò use, respectively, magazine cut-outs (especially pin-ups) and painted comic-book and advertising motifs in their work. Both have been associated with Italian groups and galleries, and, with critic Alain Jouffroy, have produced such manifestoes and environments as *Anti-Procès* and *Mecanismo*. The Germans, led by Wolf Vostell, are mainly allied with the Décollage group, whose review, published from 1962 to 1964, has printed contributions by Christo, Lebel, George Brecht, Al Hansen, Kaprow, and others. Dick Higgins, an American composer, and Nam June Paik, a Korean pianist then living in Cologne, shared the spotlight with Vostell, who did assemblages, *décollages* (lacerated posters), and television Happenings. The 'accidental' musical and theatrical orientation of the Décollage artists has also won them the approbation of John Cage. A splinter group – Fluxus – has performed its own brand of Happenings in New York and Europe. A prime example of the environmental trend was 'Dylaby', produced at the Stedelijk Museum in Amsterdam in September 1962. Six artists (Raysse, Tinguely, Saint Phalle, Ultvedt, Spoerri, and Rauschenberg) were invited to spend three weeks constructing a 'Dynamic Labyrinth' in two galleries of the museum. The result was a total or synaesthetic art recalling Kurt Schwitters' *Merzbau* construction, as well as the extravagant interior decorations of International Surrealist Exhibitions from 1938 on. In many of these demonstrations abstract kinetic art is fused with New Realism – an approach pioneered by Tinguely and, theoretically, by Klein.

The European *avant-garde* is a migratory group, with Paris the centre and increasingly large numbers shuttling between there, London, and New York. The exhibition network is widespread, and a successful artist may show in Paris, Milan, Amsterdam, Düsseldorf, and Copenhagen within a year's time. The development of influences and trends is consequently complex and uncontained by national boundaries. The American Peter Saul, who from 1956 to 1964 lived in Holland, Paris, and Rome, is a case in point. His Gorky-esque expressionist paintings with fantastic *mélanges* of Pop and Surrealist images had a pervasive influence outside the New Realist sphere, primarily on the work of Hervé Télémaque, Bernard Rancillac, and the Italians Valerio Adami and Silvio Pasotti. Rancillac made his 'animated cartoon' paintings before moving into the *nouvelle figuration* category, but Télémaque developed his own style with a strong sense

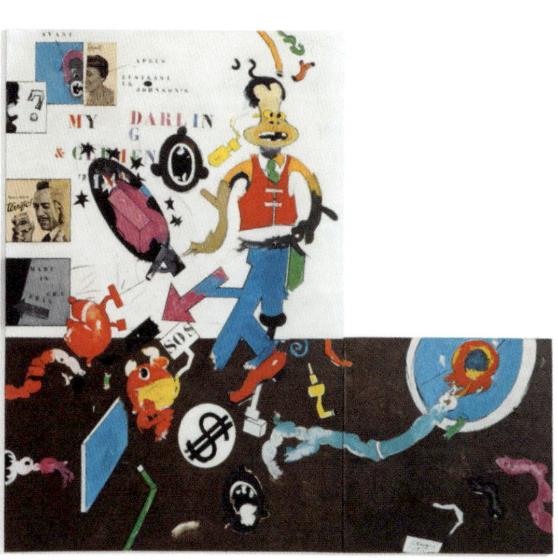

29. Hervé Télémaque, *My Darling Clementine*, 1963. Oil on canvas, glued papers, painted wooden box, rubber doll, Plexiglas of design rare in Paris. A Haitian who lived in New York in 1957–60, Télémaque's images are truly Pop, although the sources are Disney cartoons rather than the 'heavy' dramas of Lichtenstein. Télémaque's fragmented style recalls Rosenquist, Fahlström, and Allen Jones, but more important is his fusion of Anglo-American Pop and New Realism, which he achieves without relinquishing the brilliant colour and formal éclat of the former or the mysteriousness of the latter.

This is a narrative trend, based on comic-strips, rather than advertising images. Adami's iconography leans more heavily towards Surrealism than Télémaque's but for the first time a Surrealist imagery has been crystallized into a harsh commercial style. Although he worked in London and Paris in 1961–64, a 1963 painting – *Invito al Crash* – seems derived from Lichtenstein. Now Adami has evolved a distinctive style of his own – pastel colours, hard outlines, and raw patterns. A unique vocabulary of hybrid creatures – fleshy, unnamed forms and huge fingers – convey a sense of danger and sexuality all the more potent because of the rigid handling. Adami's is the typical post-Surrealist viewpoint. Metamorphosis is his goal, yet he too talks about employing 'the absolutely clear terms' of advertising art, 'understood by everybody, a language which assails you wherever you go'. Unlike his American colleagues, Adami is not concerned with formal advancement so much as a New Realism: 'The important thing,' he has written, 'is not to work out "new" visual possibilities, but to organize the reality in which we live into a narrative... . For a painter whose aim is a narrative one, it is truly difficult to define his own way of being *realist*...Time and space spread out into a new psychic action.'[42]

Aldo Mondino makes double-panel paintings of colouring-book images on graph paper – the upper panel usually just outlined, the lower one filled in with colour, the two connected by an actual box of crayons or child's paintbox attached to the surface. These have a clarity and rigour seldom seen in Italy, although the banality of the images is neither overcome nor exploited to a high degree. Mario Schifano has frequently worked in a tangential Pop style apparently based on slides, since most of his images are enclosed in round-edged rectangles on a white, screen-like ground. Around 1961–62 he used blown-up fragments of advertisements such as the Coca-Cola lettering, but rendered in a very elegant dripped and brushed style. Since then he has painted landscapes in the same manner, sometimes labelled in imitation stencil writing ('large detail of the Italian landscape in colour'), and quite Abstract Expressionist paintings including automobiles, arrows, and other commercial signs, and a series of Dine- and Rivers-like drawings of Boccioni after a famous Futurist group photograph. Schifano's choice of 'touristic' subject matter is shared by other Italians, who are not reacting against Americanization so much as against their own monumental past, which has plagued the Italian *avant-garde* since the Futurist days. Both Tano Festa and Lucio del Pezzo, while contributing nothing new to current art, take as their subjects the old masters, the magnificent architecture, and indirectly, the tourist business. In 1963–64 Festa painted a series of labelled 'slides' of Michelangelo's Sistine Chapel, and in 1965, black outlined pin-ups. Silvio Pasotti's sweetly coloured commercial images, whirling in an expressionist phantasmagoria in which the washing machine is a central image, derive from Saul, but are among the more imaginative fusions of Surrealism and Pop Art.

The man many Italians claim as the father of Pop Art is Enrico Baj, whose 'nuclear art' since 1952 bears more comparison to Dubuffet's figures or to the Chicago 'Monster School'. His rough wallpaper and furniture assemblages and his screaming generals are passionately committed and this has made him a salient figure in postwar Italy, where abstraction is largely pallid and backward-looking. His ferocious men inhabit the world of science fiction, not the down-to-earth realism of Pop Art, although he did make one series that juxtaposed grotesque little robots with highly realistic nudes copied from cheap men's magazines. The major proto-Pop painter in Italy is actually Mimmo Rotella, a charter member of Restany's Nouveaux Réalistes and one of the major exponents of the 'lacerated poster' trend. Though preceded by French *affichistes* Raymond Hains and Jacques de la Villeglé, who had been working in this medium since the 1940s, Rotella was apparently the first to use it in a Pop manner – concentrating on a single advert torn from a city wall, rather than the fragmented abstractions that they had all made before. The art of *décollage* or *affichisme* has attracted disciples in each country in Europe. Among the Italians is Alberto Moretti, whose posters are often overpainted with figures, providing a background rather than the focal point. Since Italy's walls are liberally adorned with political tracts as well as advertisements, these appear in the work of her *affichistes*, lending a touch of political satire reminiscent of Berlin Dada to the blandly smiling faces of the milk drinkers or bucolic landscapes. Giuseppe Romagnoni and Gianni Bertini have both diverged from the poster towards blurred photographic montages derived from Rauschenberg, whose acquisition of the grand prize at the 1964 Venice Biennale was a *cause célèbre* and, according to Giorgio de Marchis, established 'the revelation of North American Pop Art as an important new event'.[43]

Others working in a more or less Pop-New Realist vein in Italy are the Gruppo 70 in Florence (Luciano Ori, Alberto Moretti, Alfonso Frasnedi, Raffaele, Marisa Bonazzi), Fabio Mauri, Umberto Bignardi, Renato Mambor, Titina Maselli, Antonino Titone, Mario Ceroli, Giosetta Fioroni, Franco Angeli, Sergio Lombardo, Giuseppe Guerreschi, Giancarlo Ilifrandi, and Cesare Tacchi. Many of them use photographic techniques or images rather than commercial emblems; the most interesting of these is Michelangelo Pistoletto. His greyed figures on a highly polished metal surface, approximating mirror, change mood, scale, and composition depending on their reflected surroundings. Each of Pistoletto's paintings is potentially an infinite number of different paintings. The figures are often seen from the back or side, in casual poses, and they may be joined by a single viewer or by a whole crowd at a *vernissage*. Their appearance alters

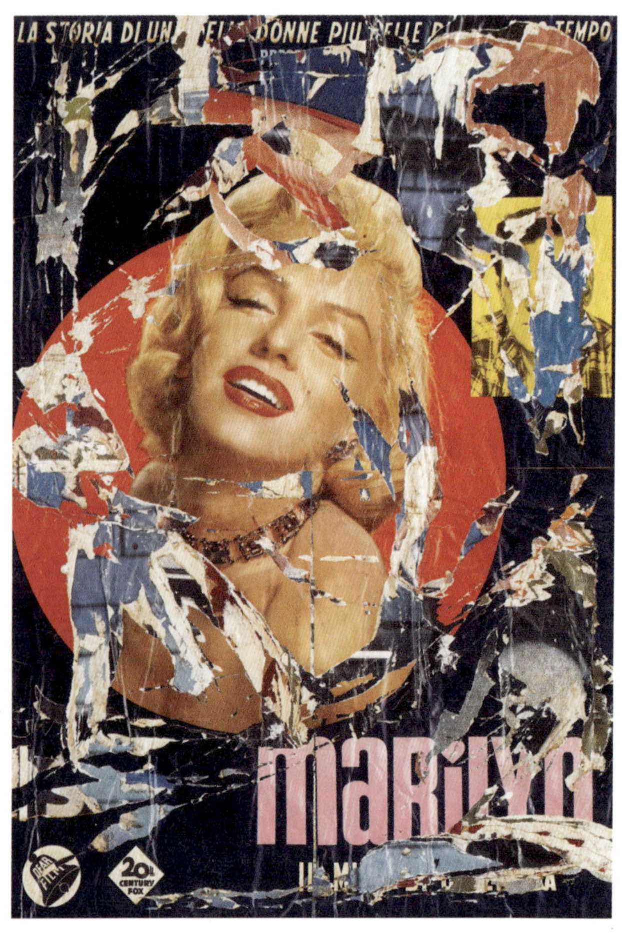

30. Mimmo Rotella, *Marilyn Monroe*, 1963.
Torn posters on canvas

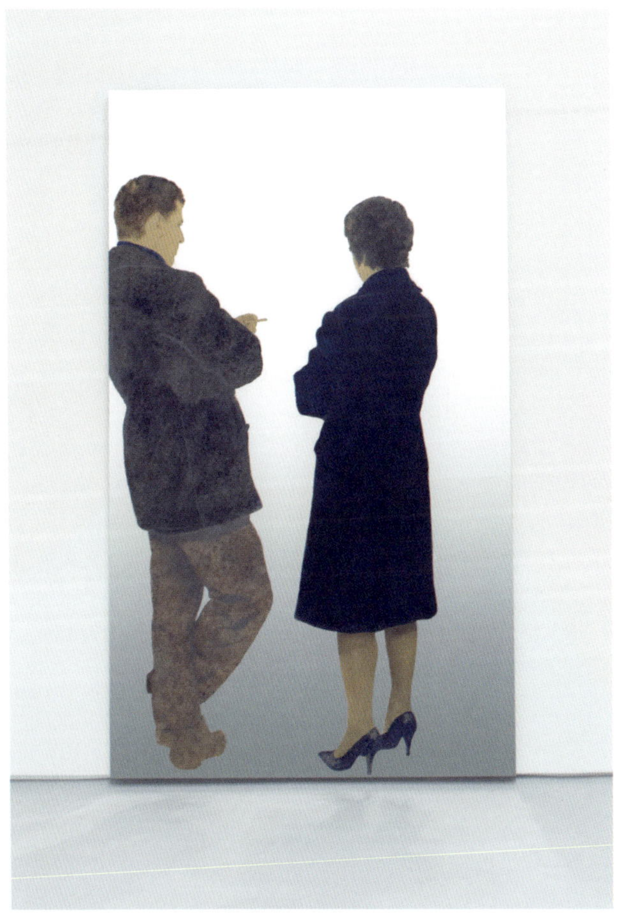

31. Michelangelo Pistoletto, *Two People*, 1963–64. Graphite and oil on cut transparent paper mounted on polished stainless steel again when they are moved from the elegance of a gallery to the clutter of a studio or the intimacy of a bedroom. They can be Realist and Surrealist. Pistoletto has written that the first real figurative experience man has is when he recognizes his own image in a mirror; in his own work, 'aesthetics and reality can be identified, but each remains in its own autonomous life.'[44]

'Quibb art is no German version of Pop Art, New Vulgarism, Junk Culture, Nouveau Réalisme or Neo-Dada,' stated H. P. Alvermann's and Winfred Gaul's *First Quibb Manifesto*, dated Düsseldorf, 30 January 1963: 'We do not work with cardboard knives. We work with a butcher's knife. Our art is no excursion to Disneyland.' Yet they also sound the note of 1960s urbanism that is common to all of the manifestations discussed here: 'Surrealism constructed its monsters. We find them on the street. We do not want to shock. The things shock us.' The objects and paintings on which these two artists collaborated, and Alvermann's own work, are vehicles of protest. The 1963 *Portrait of an Electric Pater* needs little explanation. The hostility shown toward 'good design' and the frigidity of a modern luxury life can be viewed as a particularly postwar German reaction. Gaul, however, later turned to a geometric abstraction based on traffic signals and signs which is striking in its very simple imagery and brilliant colour. Some of the 1963 paintings, such as *Verboten*, were more symbolic in their use of signs, but by 1965 Gaul had become an almost completely non-objective artist.[45] Peter Brüning, until recently an accomplished *tachiste*, makes aerial abstractions featuring targets, dotted lines, and patches of solid colour derived from road maps; Fritz Köthe, in Berlin, has made road signs surrealistically placed on lonely streets or in landscapes. The Autobahn, or super-highway, seems to play an inordinately important role in the new Germany. 'Traffic signals are omnipresent and omnipotent,' Gaul has written. 'They command and forbid. They direct us here or there.'[46]

It was in Germany that Dada had many of its most memorable moments, and the 'new objectivity' of Pop Art would seem to be appealing to the Teutonic mind. Nevertheless, as John Anthony Thwaites has pointed out: 'Pop Art proper exists in Germany only in the world of its epigones. Quite possibly, Pierre Restany is right: Pop is a product of the megalopolis, and since the loss of Berlin, Germany has no super-cities to inspire it.'[47]

Konrad Lueg and Gerhard Richter, however, who collaborated in 1963 on an event called 'Demonstration for Capitalist Realism', can really be called Pop, if not very original Pop. Both utilize the photographic image, Richter in a fast-motion, out-of-focus manner that owes something to Francis Bacon as well as to the Futurists, and Lueg in a stylized negative-positive reduction also used by the American Robert Stanley. Sigmar Polke makes black-and-white paintings derived from Roy Lichtenstein. The Swiss artist Peter Staemphli paints common objects and advertising scenes in a totally Pop deadpan style, and his compatriots Eric Beynon and Samuel Buri should also be noted. Finally, Konrad Klapheck of Düsseldorf occupies a unique position which is tangentially related to Pop. His precisely painted pipes and machines return to Léger and Picabia for inspiration, but have a curiously contemporary austerity and impersonal mien. He started painting machines as a student in 1965, beginning with typewriters, and now, by subtle distortions of parts or close-ups of details, has created his own style and image reflecting the cold materialism of an urban society.

The entire picture of European New Realism would demand a book of its own to describe. There are various isolated figures and small groups of Pop-oriented artists in every country, among them the Benelux group in Holland and Belgium, which includes Assemblagists like Vic Gentils, Hans van Eck, Paul von Hoeydonck, Michel Ansel Cardenas, Woody van Amen, and Wim Schippers. Pol Mara (Belgium) has made photographic paintings of timely subject matter. Sweden has been highly receptive to American Pop Art, and undoubtedly there are artists throughout Scandinavia who are not widely published but should be included in a full coverage of the subject. Jan Hendrikse in Curaçao, Ushio Shinohara, Nobuaki Kojima, and Keiichi Tanaami in Japan,[48] Sansegundo, René Bertholo, and Lourdes Castro of Spain and Portugal and many Latin Americans could be included in a broad survey, to say nothing of the Americans and British who are not Pop but are 'New Realistically' inclined. Many artists have exhibited or their works have been reproduced so little that they are not known abroad. Suffice it to say that the European scene is a lively and a varied one. If many younger artists are making their pilgrimages to New York and London, it is not because the European cities are

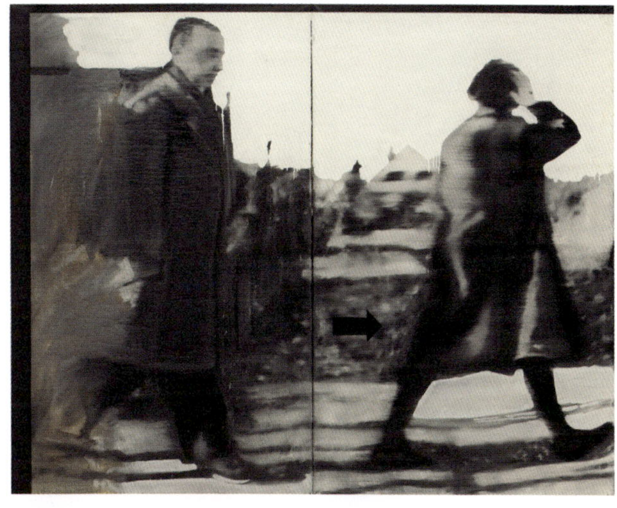

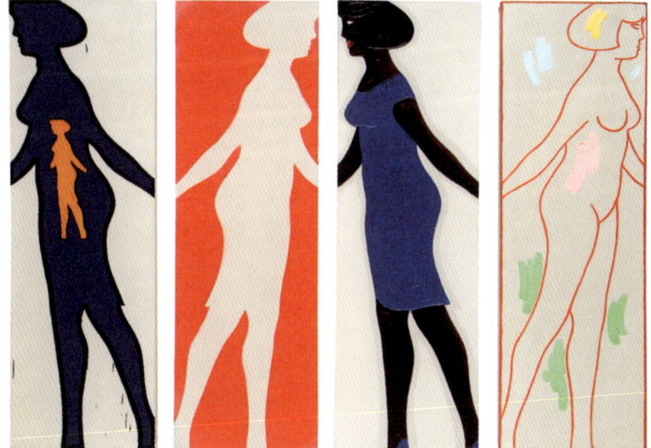

32. Gerhard Richter, *Pedestrians (Fußgänger)*, 1963. Oil on canvas
33. Michael Snow, *Four Grey Panels and Four Figures,* 1963. Oil on canvas

provincial, but because the art world has always needed a headquarters. Art feeds on art, and 'New Realities' are discovered only by art.

Canadian artists also tend to gravitate toward America. Despite the fact that it is an affluent, partially Anglo-Saxon nation, it lacks the urban concentration that is necessary not only to Pop, but to any active *avant-garde*. All of these artists are from Toronto – the heart of the central Canadian art world; it was there, at the David Mirvish Gallery, in October 1963, that the first full-scale Pop exhibition in Canada took place. The Mirvish show included Americans and English, and can be considered a significant exposure.

Armand Flint is the only prototypal Pop artist I know of in Canada. His *The Queen and Sherbourne*, with its Sweet Caporal advertisement, speech balloon and comic-strip 'Zip!', was painted in 1950, and shown that year at the Art Gallery of Toronto. It was also the last painting Flint did for almost ten years, and when he resumed, his style, while still incorporating bold numbers, was less popularly oriented. Michael Snow, Canada's best-known tangential Pop artist, first employed his ubiquitous Walking Woman motif in a cut-out form in the autumn of 1960; since then he has manipulated this 'mass produced' image in innumerable ways, steadfastly rejecting any particular 'personal' style in favour of the variety suggested by that single figure. Many of Snow's paintings are strictly Pop; an equal number are not. 'Repetition; trademark, my trade, my mark,' he has written. 'Mock mass production? Art the only "cottage industry" left.'[49]

Actually, such mockery is the least important part of Snow's ideas. He has solved for himself a dilemma about figure painting after 'several years of worrying about where the figure is or could be or would be...by removing the figure from *where* and putting it *here*, on the wall or in the room'.[50] The Walking Woman has since been taken out on the street, into the subway, cast in metal, dressed and undressed, swelled and shrunk; she has acted in films, and still has a future. She is, typically, in a hurry, and despite the Dada aspects of her career, she is basically a product of modern commercialism. So are the lip paintings of Sunao Urata, whose show at the Jerrold Morris Galleries, in May 1965, was titled 'Acrylic Kisses'. Groups of small panels, many adorned with identical images of disembodied lips in various 'lipstick' shades, benefitted from the inventive range of cosmetic colours and from the blatant eroticism of subject matter and harsh treatment. Frankly synthetic, they were made according to the Warhol principle of mass production: the panels cost $60 each, but bargain prices applied if more than one was purchased. 'Everything is so clean and icy and slick, the lips and the lipsticks are sensuously full, the colours subtly lush, like a hothouse seen through sunglasses,' wrote one impressed reviewer. 'The effect is rampant decay, suddenly arrested by refrigeration.'[51]

If Pop Art had not come along, Joyce Wieland would probably have been using the same devices with the same kind of wit anyway. A film-maker in her own right, since around 1963 she has been exploiting a sequential film or comic-strip scheme for her compartmented paintings,

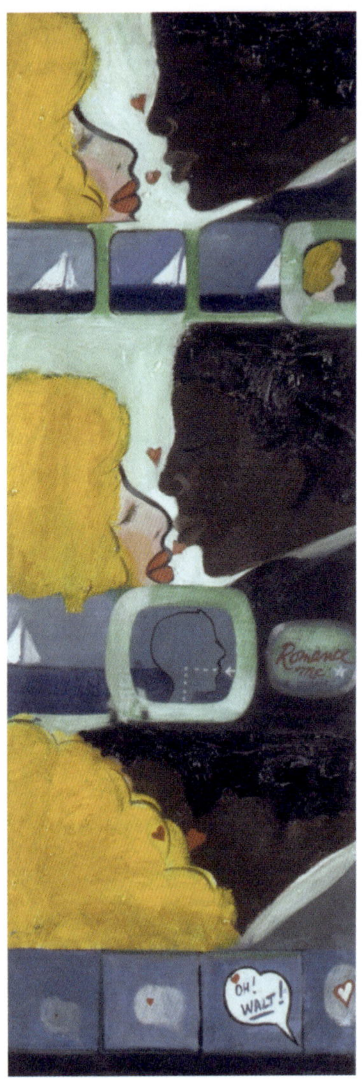

34. Joyce Wieland, *First Integrated Film with a Short on Sailing*, 1963. Oil on canvas many of which deal with disaster – crashing planes, sinking ships – and sex. The rendering is not slick, like that of hard-core Pop, and she frequently works in construction, or assemblage, as well. *Young Woman's Blues* has a photograph of Elizabeth Taylor wrapped around a beer can inside a heart-shaped box, as a plane wings its way off. *The First Integrated Film, with a Short on Sailing* depicts three cliché steps of a kiss between a blonde white girl and a Black man; the frames are separated by a charming *non-sequitur* of a sailboat moving along. About her disasters, Wieland has written from New York: 'There is the American fascination with disaster and grotesque happenings, in the newspapers and on TV, for instance, and it has come out in the work I've been doing.'[52]

Les Levine, also in New York now, has turned from his 'New Realist' heaps of furniture tightly shrouded in plastic to what he calls 'small environments' of movable plastic-masked objects set into shallow boxes – all of which is reminiscent of Christo rather than of Pop Art. Other Toronto artists bear more relation to the British brand of Pop, such as Dennis Burton's unequivocal enlargements of breasts or spread legs, which owe something to Allen Jones. Gordon Rayner's subject matter is more ambiguous; Greg Curnoe's main connection with Pop Art is his flat rendering of figures and the frequent but unobtrusive 'caption' across the top, but he has treated more popular subjects in a looser style, such as *The Greatest Profile in the World*. If there are other Pop artists in Canada, they have not yet emerged internationally.

NOTES

1 *Collage*, No. 3–4, 1965.
2 *Modern Art in Advertising* (Art Institute of Chicago, 1945), pp. 4–5.
3 'The New Realism Goes On', *Art Front* (New York), February 1937, pp. 7–8.
4 'A New Realism – The Object', *The Little Review* (New York), Winter 1926, pp. 7–8.
5 'Where Are We Going and What Are We Doing?', *Silence* (Middletown, 1961), p. 222.
6 Walter Hopps, 'An Interview with Jasper Johns', *Artforum*, March 1965, p. 35.
7 John Rublowsky, *Pop Art* (New York, 1965), p. 61; and Bruce Glaser, 'Pop Art', a tape-recorded discussion on WBAI, New York, 1964; this was made with Oldenburg, Lichtenstein, and Warhol. Quotations from it are frequent in the following text and will not be further footnoted. They were taken from a transcript which was later edited by Glaser and revised with the co-operation of all the participants; the final version was published in *Artforum*, February 1966.
8 *Time*, 2 February 1962, p. 44.
9 'Franz Kline: Painter of His Own Life', *Art News* (New York), November, 1962, p. 31.
10 John Coplans, 'An Interview with Roy Lichtenstein', *Artforum*, II, No. 4 (1963), p. 31. For additional material on the Reuben Gallery group, see Lawrence Alloway's catalogue, *Eleven from the Reuben Gallery* (Solomon R. Guggenheim Museum, New York, 1965); my review of the show in *Art International*, IX, No. 3 (1965), 51; and the Bianchini Gallery's *Ten from Rutgers University* (New York, 1965–66), preface by Allan Kaprow; and, of course, Kaprow's own writings.
11 *Art News*, Summer 1961, p. 16.
12 See Lawrence Alloway's essay, above, for discussion of Smith's importance to the development of British Pop Art, and Smith's own statements in *Living Arts*, No. 1, 1963.
13 The Wesselmann and Rosenquist quotations in this paragraph are both taken from G.R. Swenson's important interviews entitled 'What is Pop Art?', published in two parts in *Art News*, LXII, No. 7 (November 1963), and No. 10 (February 1964); the participants were Dine, Indiana, Lichtenstein, Warhol, Durkee, Johns, Rosenquist, and Wesselmann.

These interviews are quoted frequently in this text and will not be further footnoted.

14 *Vogue* (New York), 1 March 1965, p. 185.

15 'A Symposium on Pop Art', *Arts* (New York), XXXVII, No. 7 (April 1963), pp. 36–45. The symposium took place at the Museum of Modern Art, New York, 13 December 1962.

16 See Lawrence Alloway's *Six Painters and The Object* (Solomon R. Guggenheim Museum, New York, 1963), p. 2.

17 Coplans, *op. cit.*, note 6.

18 See Erle Loran, 'Pop Artists or Copy Cats?', *Art News*, September 1963, pp. 48–49, 61; and 'Cézanne and Lichtenstein: Problems of "Transformation"', *Artforum*, September 1963, pp. 34–35. Richard Hamilton, in turn, enlarged a detail of a weeping girl's head and called it *A Little Bit of Roy Lichtenstein*. This could have been carried still further if he had worked from a Lichtenstein 'Picasso'.

19 Leo Steinberg, in 'A Symposium on Pop Art' (see note 15).

20 *Americans 1963* (Museum of Modern Art, New York, 1963), pp. 74–75. Reprinted from the Martha Jackson Gallery's *Environments, Situations, Spaces*, 1961.

21 *Newsweek*, 9 November 1964, p. 96.

22 *Prospectus aux amateurs de tout genre* (Paris, 1946).

23 Boris Lurie, 'Anti-Pop', mimeographed manifesto on the occasion of his No-Poster exhibition, Gallery Gertrude Stein, New York, February 1964.

24 Michelle Stuart, 'No is an Involvement', *Artforum*, September 1963, p. 36.

25 Lawrence Alloway, *Jim Dine* (Martha Jackson Gallery, New York, 1962).

26 *Americans 1963* (see note 18).

27 'New Talent', *Art in America*, L, No. 1 (1962), p. 37.

28 'The Artists Say', *Art Voices* (New York), Summer 1965, p. 62.

29 Quoted in Rublowsky, *Pop Art*, p. 137.

30 *Art News*, November, 1962, p. 15.

31 Jean Reeves, interview with James Rosenquist, *Buffalo Evening News*, 19 November 1963.

32 Rosenquist's ideas do not coincide with most of the generalizations made about Pop Art in this text; his art is more complex than most and his statements more obscure. For further material on his work, see G. R. Swenson's interview, 'The F-111: An Interview with James Rosenquist', *Partisan Review*, Autumn, 1965; and my article, 'James Rosenquist; Aspects of a Multiple Art', *Artforum*, December 1965.

33 'Dissimulated Pop', *The Nation*, 30 November 1964, pp. 417–19.

34 For broader discussions of this sensibility, see Barbara Rose, 'ABC Art', *Art in America*, October–November 1965, pp. 57–69, and my 'The Third Stream', *Art Voices*, Spring 1965, pp. 44–49.

35 See *Mythologies Quotidiennes*, catalogue of an exhibition at the Musée d'Art Moderne, Paris, July–October 1964.

36 'The Avant-Garde Stance', *Arts*, XXXIX, No. 9 (May–June 1965), p. 22.

37 *Yves Klein* (Alexander Iolas Gallery, New York, 5–24 November 1962).

38 *Arman* (Stedelijk Museum, Amsterdam, September–November 1964).

39 'A Game of Character', *Art and Literature*, No. 3 (1964), p. 225.

40 'Oyvind Fahlström', *ibid.*, p. 219.

41 'The Snare-Picture as Picture, Spectacle and Interrogation', typescript, December 1961–December 1962.

42 *Adami* (Galleria Schwarz, Milan, October–November 1965).

43 'The Significance of the 1964 Venice Biennale', *Art International*, VIII, No. 9 (1964), p. 21.

44 *Pistoletto* (Gian Enzo Sperone arte moderna, Turin, October, 1964).

45 See Gillo Dorfles, 'I "Verkehrszeichen und Signale" di Gaul', *Art International*, IX, No. 3 (1965), pp. 30–33.

46 Quoted in Rolf-Günter Dienst, *Pop Art* (Wiesbaden, 1965), p. 91.

47 John Anthony Thwaites, 'Germany: Prophets without Honor', *Art in America*, LIII, No. 6 (December, 1965), pp. 110–15.

48 See Ichiro Hariu, 'Pop Art in Japan', *Art Voices* (Autumn 1965), pp. 50–53.

49 The artist, quoted in Arnold Rockman, 'Michael Snow and His Walking Woman', *Canadian Art* (November–December 1963), pp. 345–47.

50 *Ibid.*

51 Barrie Hale, 'Love Stifled and Kisses Cool ... In Acrylic', *The Telegram* (Toronto), 22 May 1965, p. 22.

52 *Canadian Art* (September–October 1964), p. 278.

LIST OF ILLUSTRATIONS

Measurements are given height before width, cm followed by inches

1. Robert Rauschenberg, *Coca-Cola Plan*, 1958. Graphite on paper, oil on three Coca-Cola bottles, wood newel cap and cast metal wings on wood structure, 67.9 × 64.1 × 12.1 (26¾ × 25¼ × 4¾). The Panza Collection. The Museum of Contemporary Art, Los Angeles. © Robert Rauschenberg Foundation/VAGA at ARS, NY and DACS 2024 **2.** Robert Rauschenberg, *Overdrive*, 1963. Oil and silkscreen ink on canvas, 213.4 × 152.4 (84 × 60). Private Collection. © Robert Rauschenberg Foundation/VAGA at ARS, NY and DACS 2024 **3.** Jasper Johns, *Flag*, 1954–55. Encaustic, oil, and collage on fabric mounted on plywood, three panels, 107.3 × 153.8 (42¼ × 60⅝). The Museum of Modern Art, New York. Photo The Museum of Modern Art, New York/Scala, Florence. © Jasper Johns/VAGA at ARS, NY and DACS, London 2024 **4.** H.C. Westermann, *Pillar of Truth*, 1962. Red oak, pine, walnut, enamel, cast aluminum, metal spring, 62.5 × 19.1 × 20.3 (24⅝ × 7½ × 8). Private collection. Photo Courtesy Venus Over Manhattan, New York. © Dumbarton Arts, LLC/VAGA at ARS, NY and DACS, London 2024 **5.** Robert Indiana, *Moon*, 1960. Acrylic gesso on wood beam with wood-and-iron wheels and concrete, 198.1 × 43.5 × 26 (78 × 17¼ × 10¼). The Museum of Modern Art, New York. Photo The Museum of Modern Art, New York/Scala, Florence. © Morgan Art Foundation Ltd. / Artists Rights Society (ARS), New York, DACS, London 2024 **6.** Richard Smith, *Quartet*, 1964. Oil on canvas, 168.3 × 182.9 × 50.2 (66¼ × 72 × 19¾). Walker Art Center, Minneapolis. © Richard Smith Foundation **7.** George Brecht, *Repository*, 1961. Wall cabinet containing pocket watch, thermometer, plastic and rubber balls, baseball, plastic persimmon, 'Liberty' statuette, wood puzzle, toothbrushes, bottlecaps, house number, plastic worm, pocket mirror, lightbulbs, keys, hardware, and photographs, 102.6 × 26.7 × 7.7 (40⅜ × 10½ × 3⅛). The Museum of Modern Art, New York. Photo The Museum of Modern Art, New York/Scala, Florence. © DACS 2024 **8.** Yayoi Kusama, *Air Mail Stickers*, 1962. Collaged paper on canvas, 182.6 × 172.4 (71⅞ × 67⅞). Whitney Museum of American Art, New York. © YAYOI KUSAMA 9. Jasper Johns, *The Critic Sees*, 1961. Sculp-metal on plaster with glass, 8 × 17 × 5 (3⅛ × 6½ × 2⅛). Photo courtesy Matthew Marks Gallery. © Jasper Johns/VAGA at ARS, NY and DACS, London 2024 **10.** Andy Warhol, *Campbell's Soup Cans*, 1962. Acrylic with metallic enamel paint on canvas, 32 panels, each canvas

50.8 × 40.6 (20 × 16). The Museum of Modern Art, New York. Photo The Museum of Modern Art, New York/Scala, Florence. © 2024 The Andy Warhol Foundation for the Visual Arts, Inc./Licensed by DACS, London **11.** Roy Lichtenstein, *Big Painting No. 6*, 1965. Acrylic and oil on canvas, 233 × 328 (91¾ × 129¼). Kunstsammlung Nordrhein-Westfalen, Düsseldorf. © Estate of Roy Lichtenstein/DACS 2024 **12.** Roy Lichtenstein, *As I Opened Fire...*, 1964. Acrylic, oil, graphite pencil on canvas, each panel 174 × 143.5 (68⅝ × 56½). Stedelijk Museum Amsterdam. Photo SuperStock/DeAgostini. © Estate of Roy Lichtenstein/DACS 2024 **13.** Peter Saul, *Society*, 1964. Oil on canvas, 199.4 × 189.9 (78½ × 74¾). Private Collection. © Peter Saul/ARS, New York and DACS, London 2024 **14.** Andy Warhol, *Campbell's Tomato Juice Box, Del Monte Peach Halves Box, Heinz Tomato Ketchup Box, Kellog's Cornflakes Box, Mott's Apple Juice Box, White Brillo Box, Yellow Brillo Box*, 1964. Synthetic polymer paint and screenprint on wood, dimensions variable. Private Collection. Photo Giorgio Morara/Alamy. © 2024 The Andy Warhol Foundation for the Visual Arts, Inc./Licensed by DACS, London **15.** Marisol, *John Wayne*, 1963. Wood, mixed media, 243.8 × 264.2 × 38.1 (96 × 104 × 15). Colorado Springs Fine Arts Center at Colorado College. Photo Jack Mitchell/Getty Images. © Estate of Marisol/ARS, NY and DACS, London 2024 **16.** Sam Goodman, *The Bomb*, 1960–61. Found Objects, 193 × 121.9 × 58.4 (76 × 48 × 23). Boris Lurie Art Foundation, Clifton, NJ. Courtesy of the Boris Lurie Art Foundation **17.** Claes Oldenburg, *Floor Burger*, 1962. Canvas filled with foam rubber and cardboard boxes, painted with acrylic paint, 132.1 × 226.1 (52 × 89). Art Gallery of Ontario, Toronto. Photo Art Gallery of Ontario/Bridgeman Images. © The Estate of Claes Oldenburg **18.** Claes Oldenburg, *Bedroom Ensemble*, 1963/1995. Wood, vinyl, metal, synthetic fur, muslin, dacron, polyurethane foam and lacquer. Overall 518.2 × 640.1 (204 × 252). Whitney Museum of American Art, New York. Photo Whitney Museum of American Art/Licensed by Scala. © The Estate of Claes Oldenburg **19.** Tom Wesselmann, *Great American Nude No. 48*, 1963. Oil and collage on canvas, acrylic and collage on board, enameled radiator and assemblage, 213.3 × 271.1 × 102.8 (84 × 106¾ × 40½). Private Collection. © Estate of Tom Wesselmann/VAGA at ARS, NY and DACS, London 2024 **20.** James Rosenquist, *The Lines Were Deeply Etched on the Map of Her Face*, 1962. Oil on canvas, 167.6 × 198.1 (66 × 78). Collection of Meryl and Robert Meltzer. © 2024 James Rosenquist Foundation/Licensed by Artists Rights Society (ARS), NY. Used by permission. All rights reserved **21.** Robert Indiana, *USA 666 (The Sixth American Dream)*, 1964–66. Oil on canvas, each panel 129.5 × 129.5 (51 × 51). Private Collection. © Morgan Art Foundation Ltd./Artists Rights Society (ARS), New York, DACS,

ALSO AVAILABLE IN THE POCKET PERSPECTIVES SERIES:

Julian Bell on Painting

John Boardman on The Parthenon

T. J. Clark on Bruegel

E. H. Gombrich on Fresco Painting

James Hall on The Self-Portrait

Linda Nochlin on The Body

Griselda Pollock on Gauguin

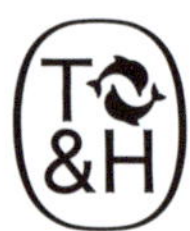

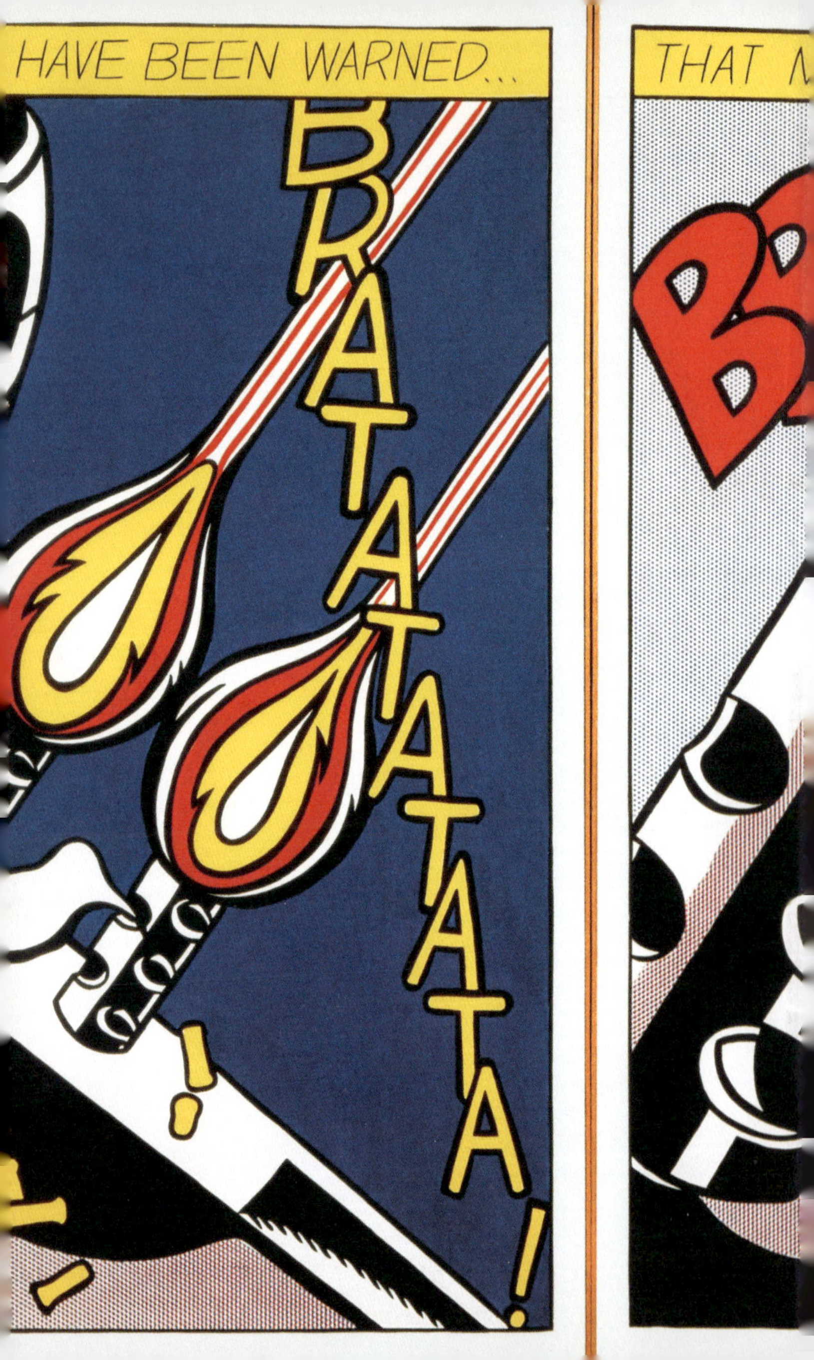

HAVE BEEN WARNED...

BRATATATATA!

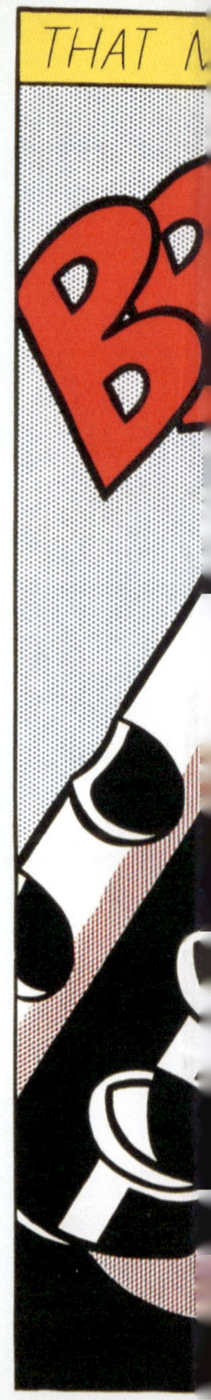